Houghton Mifflin

Mathematics

Assessment Guide

- **Prerequisite Skills Entry Test**
- **Chapter Pretests**
- **Chapter Tests**
- **Quarterly Tests**
- **End-of-Year Test**

4

HOUGHTON MIFFLIN

BOSTON • MORRIS PLAINS, NJ

California • Colorado • Georgia • Illinois • New Jersey • Texas

Contents

Introduction to Assessment

✳ Assessing student knowledge is an essential part of instruction. Educators agree that the primary purpose of assessment is to promote learning. Through assessment tools, teachers are able to determine the skills and level of mastery students have achieved and to use these findings to promote understanding of mathematical concepts. Houghton Mifflin Mathmatics provides a variety of assessment options both within the student edition (Quick Checks for Progress Monitoring, Chapter Reviews, Chapter Tests) and in the Assessment Guide.

✳ The assessment items included in this Assessment Guide will give you a broad picture of students' understanding of mathematical processes, skills, and concepts. The different types of tests found in this guide will help you assess students' prior knowledge, evaluate whether students have acquired knowledge of new content, and determine whether students are prepared to go on to new chapters. You will also be able to assess students' understanding of concepts and skills that span a three-chapter range with quarterly tests and students' mastery of the entire year of mathematical instruction and grade-level objectives. Student Record Sheets are also provided to help you keep track of students' performance and to make it easier to evaluate whether chapter objectives are met.

✳ These assessment tools can also help you tailor your lessons to your students needs. You can use them as review tools to refresh and reinforce prior knowledge. The information gleaned from these assessment tools can also guide you to reteach concepts that students have not yet mastered and to emphasize skills and concepts that students exhibit weaknesses in.

✳ The purpose of assessment is to help teachers become more aware of what students can do, and to determine what would improve learning and understanding. This Assessment Guide provides the assessment tools to achieve this goal.

Assessment Guide Overview

Entry Level Tests

Inventory Test This test assesses knowledge of objectives and skills taught in the previous grade. It indicates whether students are prepared to learn new content and identifies which mathematical skills are lacking.

Chapter Pretests There are two sections to each Chapter Pretest. The first section, Do You Remember?, assesses prerequisite skills needed in order to be able to master the content in the upcoming chapter. The second section, Try These!, assesses knowledge of content to be presented in the new chapter. Both the prerequisite skills and the new content being tested are identified in the Assessment and suggestions and materials.

Summative Tests

Chapter Tests The Chapter Tests, Forms A and B, assess the chapter objectives and can be used to determine which objectives students have mastered. Both tests include the same items. The Form A Test uses a free-response format. The Form B Test uses a multiple choice format.

You can use the **Student Record Sheet**, one for each chapter, to record students' performance on these tests. Chapter objectives are listed on the Student Record Sheets.

Quarterly Tests Quarterly Tests cover content for three-chapter blocks (Chapters 1-3, 4-6, 7-9, and 10-12). These tests allow you to assess how well students have mastered skills and objectives from the preceding three chapters. Quarterly Tests are not cumulative. Quarterly Tests use a multiple choice format. You can use the Student Record Sheet, one for each test, to record students' performance.

End-of-Year Test The End-of-Year Test covers the content of all chapters, 1 through 12. This test gives you a broad look at how well students have mastered the content covered over the course of the year. The End-of-Year Test uses a free-response format.

Performance Assessment (Grades 1 and 2) Performance Assessment allows you to determine students' mastery of mathematical skills and concepts through activities that reflect application of mathematics to real-life situations. A Performance Assessment task is provided for each chapter at Grades 1 and 2. (Performance Assessments are included in the Student Editions at Grades 3-6.) A 4-point Scoring Rubric is provided for each Performance Assessment.

Name _____ Date _____

Write the correct answer.

1. Round the number to the underlined digit.

   7,5̲62   _____

---

2. Write the numbers in order from least to greatest.

   2,834   2,384   2,482   _____

---

3. Write the amount, using a $ sign and a decimal point.

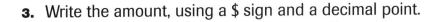

    _____

---

4. What time is it?

                                        _____

---

5. Add.   3,248
           + 1,483

6. Subtract.   5,581
               − 2,368

---

7. Find the missing measure.

   6 pt = _____ qt

Name _____ Date _____

8. Which unit would you use to measure the mass of a horse—a gram or a kilogram?

_____

9. Write a multiplication sentence for the array.

_____

Multiply.

10. $10 \times 5 =$ _____

11. $6 \times 4 =$ _____

12. $3 \times 3 \times 5 =$ _____

13. Write the special name of the figure.

_____

14. Do the figures appear to be congruent?

_____

 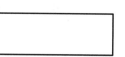

Divide.

15. $36 \div 9 =$ _____

16. $58 \div 1 =$ _____

17. $27 \div 3 =$ _____

18. Write the complete fact family for 7×4.

_____ _____ _____ _____

Name _____   Date _____

Write the correct answer.

19. Mark the point (4, 2) on the grid.

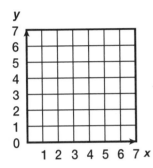

20. Use the spinner.

Is it *certain, likely,* or *impossible* that the first spin will land on gray?

_____

21. Write a fraction for the shaded part.

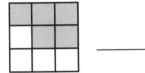   _____

22. Write the fractions in order from least to greatest.

$\frac{1}{4}$ $\frac{1}{3}$ $\frac{1}{6}$ _____

23. Add.   0.65
                 $+\,0.19$

24. Multiply.   256
                    $\times\ \ 4$

25. Divide. $4\overline{)656}$

Name _____ Date _____

Do you remember?

1. Write the number one thousand, three hundred fifty-six in standard form. _____

2. Write 103 in word form. _____

3. Write 6,594 in word form. _____

4. Write the value of the digit 7 in the number 7,301. _____

5. Round 427 to the nearest ten. _____

6. Round 648 to the nearest hundred. _____

7. Round 5,809 to the nearest hundred. _____

8. Round 2,513 to the nearest thousand. _____

Compare. Write >, <, or = in each ◯.

9. 684 ◯ 486

10. 921 ◯ 927

11. 6,403 ◯ 6,403

12. 5,172 ◯ 4,982

Write the total value.

13. 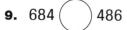 _____

14.    _____

Name _____ Date _____

Try These!

15. Write the number twenty-one thousand, eight hundred fifty
in standard form. _____

16. Write 16,324 in word form.

_____

Compare. Write >, < , or = in each ◯.

17. 168,000 ◯ 158,000

18. 92,457 ◯ 92,531

Round each number to the place of the underlined digit.

19. 6<u>2</u>0,499 _____

20. <u>4</u>89,127 _____

Write each number in another way.

21. 500,000 + 4,000 + 200 + 6

_____

22. fourteen thousand, nine hundred eighty _____

Write the value of the underlined digit.

23. 1<u>2</u>7,413,526 _____

24. <u>6</u>24,985,317 _____

Compare. Write >, < , or = in each ◯.

25. 31,416,528 ◯ 314,165,280

26. 1,840,920 ◯ 1,804,920

Round each number to the place of the underlined digit.

27. 12,<u>0</u>54,935 _____

28. 983,<u>0</u>97,115 _____

Name _____ Date _____

Write each amount. Circle which is greater.

29.

  _____

  _____

A $20 bill was used to buy each item below.
List the coins and bills you would use to make change.

30. cost of item: $15.55

_____

31. cost of item: $12.75

_____

Name _____   Date _____

Write the correct answers.

1. Write the expanded form of 6,340.

   _____

2. Write the word form of 356.

   _____

3. Write the word form of 9,020,000.

   _____

4. Write the standard form of *twenty thousand, three hundred, four.*

   _____

5. Write the standard form of *six hundred thirty-six million, eighty-five thousand, forty.*

   _____

6. What is the value of the digit 5 in 451,392?

   _____

7. What is the value of the digit 8 in 528,641,037?

   _____

Compare. Write >, < , *or* = *in each* ◯.

8. 398 ◯ 389

9. 8,265 ◯ 8,756

10. 435,040 ◯ 435,040

11. 617,429,856 ◯ 628,914,256

Name _____ Date _____

12. Write the numbers in order from greatest to least.

1,624   1,264   2,146

_____

13. Write the numbers in order from least to greatest.

859,143   897,289   889,998

_____

14. Write the numbers in order from least to greatest.

20,617,429,856   20,671,924,576   20,628,914,256

_____

15. Round 4,712 to the nearest hundred.

_____

16. Round 87,921 to the nearest thousand.

_____

17. Round 4,706,427,823 to the nearest billion.

_____

18. Which place is the number rounded to?

572,148,213   ⟶   600,000,000

_____

19. Write the amount.

_____

12

Name _____ Date _____

20. Write the amount.

_____

21. Which is the greatest amount?

2 twenty-dollar bills and 2 five-dollar bills
1 twenty-dollar bill and 2 ten-dollar bills
3 twenty-dollar bills
4 ten-dollar bills and 2 five-dollar bills

_____

22. A $20 bill is used to buy an item costing $16.85. Write the correct change.

_____

23. Suppose 25,892 people attend a baseball game. To the nearest thousand, how many people attend the game?

_____

24. Mark, Jayson, Andrea, and Ashley ride their bikes to school. They park their bikes side-by-side in the bike rack. Jayson's bike is next to Mark's bike. Andrea's bike is last. Mark's bike is first. In what order do the children park their bikes?

_____

25. Yolanda earns $7 for helping her neighbor plant his garden. She uses the money to buy two books. If each book costs $2.75, how much change should she get?

_____

Name _____ Date _____

Fill in the ◯ for the correct answer.

1. What is the expanded form of 6,340?

   (A) 6 + 3 + 4

   (B) 6 + 3 + 4 + 0

   (C) 600 + 30 + 4

   (D) 6,000 + 300 + 40

2. What is the word form of 356?

   (F) three hundred fifty-six

   (G) three five six

   (H) three hundred and fifty-six

   (J) 6 hundred 35

3. What is the word form of 9,020,000?

   (A) nine thousand, twenty

   (B) nine million, twenty

   (C) nine million, twenty thousand

   (D) nine million, two hundred thousand

4. What is the standard form of *twenty thousand, three hundred four?*

   (F) 234   (G) 20,034   (H) 20,304   (J) 20,340

5. What is the standard form of *six hundred thirty-six million, eighty-five thousand, forty?*

   (A) 636,085,040   (B) 636,850,040   (C) 636,850,400   (D) 636,854,000

6. What is the value of the digit 5 in 451,392?

   (F) 500,000

   (G) 50,000

   (H) 5,000

   (J) 500

7. What is the value of the digit 8 in 528,641,037?

   (A) 8,000,000

   (B) 800,000

   (C) 80,000

   (D) 8,000

Name _____   Date _____

Choose the symbol that makes each statement true.

8. 398 ⬤ 389

(F) >   (G) <   (H) =   (J) +

9. 8,265 ⬤ 8,756

(A) >   (B) <   (C) =   (D) +

10. 435,040 ⬤ 435,040

(F) >   (G) <   (H) =   (J) +

11. 617,429,856 ⬤ 628,914,256

(A) >   (B) <   (C) =   (D) +

12. Which is in order from greatest to least?

1,624   1,264   2,146

(F) 1,264   1,624   2,146   (G) 1,624   1,264   2,146

(H) 2,146   1,624   1,264   (J) 2,146   1,264   1,624

13. Which is in order from least to greatest?

859,143   897,289   889,998

(A) 859,143   897,289   889,998   (B) 859,143   889,998   897,289

(C) 889,998   859,143   897,289   (D) 897,289   889,998   859,143

Name _____ Date _____

14. Which is in order from least to greatest?

20,617,429,856   20,671,924,576   20,628,914,256

(F) 20,617,429,856   20,628,914,256   20,671,924,576

(G) 20,617,429,856   20,671,924,756   20,628,914,256

(H) 20,628,914,256   20,617,429,856   20,671,924,756

(J) 20,671,924,756   20,628,914,256   20,617,429,856

15. Round 4,712 to the nearest hundred.

(A) 4,700   (B) 4,710   (C) 4,720   (D) 4,800

16. Round 87,921 to the nearest thousand.

(F) 87,900   (G) 87,920   (H) 88,000   (J) 89,000

17. Round 4,706,427,823 to the nearest billion.

(A) 4,000,000,000

(B) 4,707,000,000

(C) 4,708,000,000

(D) 5,000,000,000

18. Which place is the number rounded to?

572,148,213 ⟶ 600,000,000

(F) hundred millions   (G) hundred thousands

(H) millions   (J) thousands

19. Which is the amount shown?

(A) $0.90   (B) $0.93   (C) $0.98   (D) $1.03

Name _____ Date _____

20. Which is the amount shown?

F) $40.15

G) $45.75

H) $50.15

J) $50.75

21. Which is the greatest amount?

A) 2 twenty-dollar bills and 2 five-dollar bills

B) 1 twenty-dollar bill and 2 ten-dollar bills

C) 3 twenty-dollar bills

D) 4 ten-dollar bills and 2 five-dollar bills

22. A $20 bill is used to buy an item costing $16.85. Which is the correct change?

F) 1 nickel, 1 dime, 3 one-dollar bills

G) 1 nickel, 1 dime, 4 one-dollar bills

H) 1 dime, 3 quarters, 4 one-dollar bills

J) 1 dime, 3 quarters, 3 one-dollar bills

Name _____ Date _____

23. Suppose 25,892 people attend a baseball game.
To the nearest thousand, how many people attend the game?

(A) 30,000

(B) 26,000

(C) 25,000

(D) 20,000

24. Mark, Jayson, Andrea, and Ashley ride their bikes to school. They park their bikes side-by-side in the bike rack. Jayson's bike is next to Mark's bike. Andrea's bike is last. Mark's bike is first. In what order do the children park their bikes?

(F) Mark, Jayson, Andrea, Ashley

(G) Mark, Ashley, Jayson, Andrea

(H) Mark, Jayson, Ashley, Andrea

(J) Mark, Ashley, Andrea, Jayson

25. Yolanda earns $7 for helping her neighbor plant his garden. She uses the money to buy two books. If each book costs $2.75, how much change should she get?

(A) $2.00

(B) $1.50

(C) $1.00

(D) $0.50

Name _____   Date _____

Do you remember?

Add or subtract.

1. 4 + 3 _____

2. 6 + 9 _____

3. 8 + 4 _____

4. 7 + 9 _____

5. 6 + 5 _____

6. 2 + 7 _____

7. 3 + 5 _____

8. 9 + 8 _____

9. 14 − 8 _____

10. 12 − 9 _____

11. 9 − 1 _____

12. 14 − 9 _____

13. 8 − 2 _____

14. 17 − 4 _____

15. 13 − 6 _____

16. 19 − 10 _____

17. 45 + 38 _____

18. 236 − 59 _____

19. 768 + 141 _____

20. 537 − 285 _____

21.
$$\begin{array}{r} 76 \\ +\ 67 \\ \hline \end{array}$$

22.
$$\begin{array}{r} 46 \\ +\ 19 \\ \hline \end{array}$$

23.
$$\begin{array}{r} 123 \\ +599 \\ \hline \end{array}$$

24.
$$\begin{array}{r} 456 \\ +\ 75 \\ \hline \end{array}$$

25.
$$\begin{array}{r} 52 \\ -24 \\ \hline \end{array}$$

26.
$$\begin{array}{r} 44 \\ -25 \\ \hline \end{array}$$

27.
$$\begin{array}{r} 311 \\ -199 \\ \hline \end{array}$$

28.
$$\begin{array}{r} 675 \\ -598 \\ \hline \end{array}$$

Name _____ Date _____

Try These!

Complete each number sentence. Tell which property of addition you used.

29. $32 + 56 =$ _____ $+ 32$ _____

30. $(15 + 6) + 7 = 15 + (6 +$ _____$)$ _____

31. $999 + 0 =$ _____ _____

Add or subtract.

32.	1,146 + 876	33.	2,397 + 1,439	34.	2,447 + 556	35.	8,392 + 177
36.	1,817 + 993	37.	3,912 + 1,487	38.	2,333 + 5,678	39.	7,227 + 8,349
40.	1,246 − 347	41.	5,231 − 3,863	42.	34,721 − 29,719	43.	24,322 − 17,853
44.	40,000 − 30,941	45.	10,400 − 8,231	46.	12,500 − 12,098	47.	3,006 − 239

Round each number to the nearest hundred. Estimate the sum or difference.

48.	6,893 + 542	49.	4,251 − 1,294
50.	25,989 + 36,146	51.	8,973 − 2,613

Name _____ Date _____

Write the correct answer for each.

1. Group or rearrange the addends so that you can add mentally.
   Then find the sum.

   234 + 492 + 8   _____

2. Complete the number sentence. Which property of addition did
   you use?

   14 + 37 = _____ + 14   _____

3. 456
   + 235

4. 979
   + 1,112

5. 16,982
   + 24,218

6. 532
   − 186

7. 12,917
   − 3,828

8. 2,563
   − 275

9. Round each number to the nearest ten. Then estimate.

   487 + 316 = _____

10. Round each number to the nearest dollar. Then estimate.

    $83.25 − $15.99 = _____

11. Round each to the nearest hundred. Then estimate.

    4,075 + 750 = _____

12. 103
    − 87

13. 35,000
    − 4,010

14. 5,004
    − 971

15. Simplify the expression.

    (14 + 2) + (24 − 9)   _____

Name _____ Date _____

16. Complete by choosing $>$, $<$, or $=$.

$7 + (112 - 19) \bigcirc (112 - 19) + 7$

17. Evaluate the expression when $x = 6$.

$x + 5$ _____

18. Evaluate the expression when $n = 8$.

$(n - 3) + 2$ _____

19. Solve the equation.

$r + 4 = 12$ _____

20. Solve the equation.

$t - 3 = 10$ _____

21. Find the value of y for the following equation when $x = 5$.

$y = x + 2$ _____

22. Find the value of n for the following equation when $m = 12$.

$n = m - 10$ _____

23. Pedro bought a turkey wrap for $3.75 and a small fruit juice for $1.55. About how much change should he get back from a $20 bill?

_____

24. The normal monthly temperature in June in Portland, Oregon, is 16° cooler than the normal monthly temperature in June in Mobile, Alabama. The normal monthly temperature in June in Mobile, Alabama, is 80°F. What is the normal monthly temperature in June in Portland?

_____

25. Together, Madie and Beth have 48 CDs. Beth has 8 more CDs than Madie. How many CDs does Madie have?

_____

Name _____ Date _____

Fill in the ◯ for the correct answer.

1. Group or rearrange the addends so that you can add mentally. Then find the sum.

   234 + 492 + 8

   (A) 534   (B) 634

   (C) 734   (D) 834

2. Complete the number sentence. Which property of addition did you use?

   14 + 37 = ▨ + 14

   (F) 37; Associative   (G) 37; Commutative

   (H) 37; Zero property   (J) 14; Commutative

3. 456   (A) 681
   + 235
            (B) 691

            (C) 781

            (D) 791

4.   979   (F) 2,091
   + 1,112
             (G) 2,081

             (H) 1,091

             (J) 1,081

5. 16,982   (A) 30,190
   + 24,218
             (B) 32,200

             (C) 40,200

             (D) 41,200

6. 532   (F) 456
   − 186
            (G) 445

            (H) 346

            (J) 345

7. 12,917   (A) 11,111
   − 3,828
             (B) 9,111

             (C) 9,099

             (D) 9,089

8. 2,563   (F) 2,312
   − 275
            (G) 2,288

            (H) 2,212

            (J) 288

9. Round each number to the nearest ten. Then estimate.

   487 + 316 =

   (A) 810   (B) 800   (C) 790   (D) 700

Name _____ Date _____

10. Round each number to the nearest dollar. Then estimate.

$83.25 − $15.99 =

(F) $60   (G) $64   (H) $67   (J) $68

11. Round each to the nearest hundred. Then estimate.

4,075 + 750 =

(A) 4,700   (B) 4,800   (C) 4,900   (D) 5,000

12.
$$\begin{array}{r} 103 \\ -\ 87 \\ \hline \end{array}$$

(F) 26
(G) 24
(H) 16
(J) 6

13.
$$\begin{array}{r} 35,000 \\ -\ 4,010 \\ \hline \end{array}$$

(A) 30,010
(B) 30,990
(C) 31,010
(D) 31,990

14.
$$\begin{array}{r} 5,004 \\ -\ 971 \\ \hline \end{array}$$

(F) 4,033
(G) 4,037
(H) 4,937
(J) 4,973

15. Simplify the expression.

(14 + 2) + (24 − 9)

(A) 31   (B) 29

(D) 19   (C) 21

16. Complete by choosing >, <, or =.

7 + (112 − 19) ◯ (112 − 19) + 7

(F) >   (G) <   (H) =

17. Evaluate the expression when $x = 6$.

$x + 5$

(A) 1   (B) 2

(C) 11   (D) 12

18. Evaluate the expression when $n = 8$.

$(n − 3) + 2$

(F) 3   (G) 7

(H) 9   (J) 13

Name _____ Date _____

19. Solve the equation.

$r + 4 = 12$

(A) 3   (B) 8

(C) 16   (D) 48

20. Solve the equation.

$t - 3 = 10$

(F) 13   (G) 10

(H) 7   (J) 3

21. Find the value of y for the following equation when $x = 5$.

$y = x + 2$

(A) 2   (B) 5   (C) 7   (D) 10

22. Find the value of n for the following equation when $m = 12$.

$n = m - 10$

(F) 22   (G) 12   (H) 8   (J) 2

23. Pedro bought a turkey wrap for $3.75 and a small fruit juice for $1.55. About how much change should he get back from a $20 bill?

(A) $16   (B) $14   (C) $6   (D) $4

24. The normal monthly temperature in June in Portland, Oregon, is 16° cooler than the normal monthly temperature in June in Mobile, Alabama. The normal monthly temperature in June in Mobile, Alabama, is 80°F. What is the normal monthly temperature in June in Portland?

(F) 96°F   (G) 76°F   (H) 74°F   (J) 64°F

25. Together, Madie and Beth have 48 CDs. Beth has 8 more CDs than Madie. How many CDs does Madie have?

(A) 20   (B) 28   (C) 32   (D) 40

Name _____ Date _____

Do you remember?

Multiply.

1. 6 × 3 _____

2. 5 × 5 _____

3. 9 × 6 _____

4. 3 × 8 _____

5. 7 × 5 _____

Divide.

6. 16 ÷ 4 _____

7. 27 ÷ 3 _____

8. 42 ÷ 7 _____

9. 81 ÷ 9 _____

10. 36 ÷ 4 _____

Try These!

Find each product.
Use double facts to help you.

11. 8 × 4 _____

12. 6 × 5 _____

Name _____ Date _____

Solve each equation.
Name the property you used.

13. $1 \times 45 = n$ _____

14. $(4 \times 3) \times 8 = 4 \times (n \times 8)$ _____

Find each product.

15. 10×8 _____

16. 9×8 _____

17. 7×9 _____

Find each quotient.

18. $24 \div 4$ _____

19. $36 \div 6$ _____

20. $42 \div 7$ _____

21. $45 \div 9$ _____

22. $18 \div 4$ _____

23. $53 \div 7$ _____

Solve.
If an equation has no solution, tell why.

24. $30 \div 7 = n$ _____

25. $51 \div 8 = n$ _____

26. $27 \div 1 = n$ _____

27. $5 \div 0 = n$ _____

Name _____ Date _____

Write the correct answer.

Find each product. Use double facts to help you.

1. $5 \times 10 =$ _____

2. $8 \times 6 =$ _____

Find each product.

3. $3 \times 9 =$ _____

4. $7 \times 5 =$ _____

5. $8 \times 7 =$ _____

6. $6 \times 6 =$ _____

7. Write the fact family for the set of numbers 7, 6, and 42.

_____ _____

_____ _____

Find each quotient.

8. $32 \div 8 =$ _____

9. $24 \div 6 =$ _____

10. $21 \div 3 =$ _____

11. $45 \div 5 =$ _____

Find each quotient and remainder.

12. $35 \div 8 =$ _____

13. $25 \div 4 =$ _____

Solve each equation. Name the property that you used.

14. $7 \times 3 = 3 \times m$ _____

15. $(3 \times 6) \times 5 = w \times (6 \times 5)$ _____

Name _____ Date _____

Solve.

16. $n \div 9 = 1$ _____

17. $18 \div 0 = d$ _____

Evaluate each expression when $n = 5$.

18. $3n$ _____

19. $8n - 2$ _____

Evaluate each expression when $a = 3$.

20. $18 \div a$ _____

21. $3 + 2a$ _____

Solve each equation.

22. $4a = 16$ _____

23. $7 = 14 \div m$ _____

24. Mike is collecting bugs for a science project. Mike has collected 9 bugs. Amy wants to collect three times as many bugs as Mike. How many bugs must Amy collect?

_____

25. Pamela can buy one pen for $2 or 4 pens for $5. How much will she pay for 5 pens?

_____

Name _____ Date _____

Fill in the ◯ for the correct answer.

Find each product. Use double facts to help you.

1. $5 \times 10 =$ (A) 50 (B) 15 (C) 5 (D) 2

2. $8 \times 6 =$ (F) 14 (G) 24 (H) 36 (J) 48

Find each product.

3. $3 \times 9 =$ (A) 12 (B) 18 (C) 27 (D) 36

4. $7 \times 5 =$ (F) 42 (G) 35 (H) 28 (J) 21

5. $8 \times 7 =$ (A) 15 (B) 36 (C) 48 (D) 56

6. $6 \times 6 =$ (F) 12 (G) 24 (H) 36 (J) 42

7. Find the fact family for the set of numbers 7, 6, and 42.

(A) $7 \times 6 = 42$ $6 \times 7 = 42$ $42 \div 6 = 7$ $42 \div 7 = 6$

(B) $42 \times 6 = 7$ $42 \times 7 = 6$ $42 \div 6 = 7$ $42 \div 7 = 6$

(C) $6 \times 7 = 42$ $42 \times 6 = 7$ $42 \div 7 = 6$ $7 \div 6 = 42$

(D) $42 \times 7 = 6$ $7 \times 6 = 42$ $6 \div 42 = 7$ $7 \div 6 = 42$

Find each quotient.

8. $32 \div 8 =$ (F) 16 (G) 8 (H) 4 (J) 2

9. $24 \div 6 =$ (A) 2 (B) 4 (C) 8 (D) 12

10. $21 \div 3 =$ (F) 7 (G) 14 (H) 21 (J) 63

11. $45 \div 5 =$ (A) 9 (B) 8 (C) 7 (D) 6

Find each quotient and remainder.

12. $35 \div 8 =$ (F) 5 R5 (G) 4 R3 (H) 3 R4 (J) 3 R3

13. $25 \div 4 =$ (A) 6 R1 (B) 5 R5 (C) 5 R1 (D) 4 R1

Name _____   Date _____

Solve each equation. Name the property that you used.

14. $7 \times 3 = 3 \times m$ (F) 7; Associative Property   (G) 7; Commutative Property

(H) 3; Associative Property   (J) 3; Commutative Property

15. $(3 \times 6) \times 5 = w \times (6 \times 5)$ (A) 3; Associative Property   (B) 5; Associative Property

(C) 6; Associative Property   (D) 3; Commutative Property

Solve.

16. $n \div 9 = 1$ (F) 0   (G) 1   (H) 9   (J) not possible

17. $18 \div 0 = d$ (A) 0   (B) 1   (C) 18   (D) not possible

Evaluate each expression when n = 5.

18. $3n$ (F) 3   (G) 5   (H) 8   (J) 15

19. $8n - 2$ (A) 38   (B) 20   (C) 11   (D) 9

Evaluate each expression when a = 3.

20. $18 \div a$ (F) 21   (G) 15   (H) 9   (J) 6

21. $3 + 2a$ (A) 8   (B) 9   (C) 11   (D) 13

Solve each equation.

22. $4a = 16$ (F) 12   (G) 8   (H) 4   (J) 2

23. $7 = 14 \div m$ (A) 2   (B) 7   (C) 14   (D) 28

24. Mike is collecting bugs for a science project. Mike has collected 9 bugs. Amy wants to collect three times as many bugs as Mike. How many bugs must Amy collect?

(F) 6   (G) 9   (H) 12   (J) 27

25. Pamela can buy one pen for $2 or 4 pens for $5. How much will she pay for 5 pens?

(A) $4   (B) $5   (C) $7   (D) $10

Name _____ Date _____

Find each product.

1. 8 × 8 _____

2. 3 × 8 _____

3. 4 × 7 _____

4. 7 × 7 _____

Solve each equation. Name the property you used.

5. 6 × 8 = n × 6 _____

6. (3 × 7) × 2 = n × (7 × 2) _____

7. 3 × n = 3 _____

8. 8 × n = 0 _____

Round to the greatest place.

9. 22 _____

10. 364 _____

11. 652 _____

12. 4,468 _____

Try These!

Use basic facts and patterns to find each product.

13. 6 × 4 _____

6 × 40 _____

14. 5 × 70 _____

5 × 700 _____

Find each product.

15.
$$\begin{array}{r} 79 \\ \times\ 7 \\ \hline \end{array}$$

16.
$$\begin{array}{r} 82 \\ \times\ 6 \\ \hline \end{array}$$

Name _____ Date _____

17.   368
        $\times$ 4

18.   792
        $\times$ 5

19.   6,192
        $\times$ 3

20.   8,964
        $\times$ 6

21. 204 $\times$ 8 _____

22. 5,006 $\times$ 7 _____

23. 8 $\times$ 60 _____

24. 50 $\times$ 400 _____

25. 46 $\times$ 21 _____

26. 83 $\times$ 95 _____

27. 846 $\times$ 27 _____

28. 340 $\times$ 38 _____

Estimate each product.

29. \$3.84 $\times$ 6 _____

30. 469 $\times$ 7 _____

Name _____ Date _____

Write the correct answer.

Use basic facts and patterns to find each product.

1. $3 \times 70 =$ _____

2. $6 \times 400 =$ _____

3. $8 \times 9,000 =$ _____

Find each product.

4.
$$\begin{array}{r} 43 \\ \times\ \ 6 \\ \hline \end{array}$$

5.
$$\begin{array}{r} 86 \\ \times\ \ 5 \\ \hline \end{array}$$

6.
$$\begin{array}{r} 72 \\ \times\ \ 9 \\ \hline \end{array}$$

7.
$$\begin{array}{r} 642 \\ \times\ \ 7 \\ \hline \end{array}$$

8. $3 \times \$8.46 =$ _____

9.
$$\begin{array}{r} 495 \\ \times\ \ 6 \\ \hline \end{array}$$

10.
$$\begin{array}{r} 3,894 \\ \times\ \ \ \ 8 \\ \hline \end{array}$$

11. $2 \times 4,663 =$ _____

12. $9 \times 209 =$ _____

13. $4 \times 3,008 =$ _____

14. $7 \times 7,300 =$ _____

Estimate each product.

15.
$$\begin{array}{r} 65 \\ \times\ \ 4 \\ \hline \end{array}$$

16.
$$\begin{array}{r} 788 \\ \times\ \ 5 \\ \hline \end{array}$$

17.
$$\begin{array}{r} 3,289 \\ \times\ \ \ \ 6 \\ \hline \end{array}$$

Name _____ Date _____

Multiply.

18. 40
    × 30

19. 800
    × 70

20. 36
    × 24

21. 65 × 83 = _____

22. 489 × 29 = _____

Solve.

23. Jon built 6 towers with blocks. The smallest was 4 blocks high, the next was 7 blocks high, and the third was 10 blocks high. If he continues this pattern, how many blocks high will the tallest tower be?

    _____

24. Bobby has a car collection. He has 24 cars displayed on each of 4 shelves. How many cars does he have in his collection?

    _____

25. The students at Oak Crest Elementary School raised money to donate to a local charity. If students in the fourth grade raised 3 times the amount of money students in the third grade raised, how much did the fourth grade raise?

Money Raised	
First Grade	$ $ $
Second Grade	$ $
Third Grade	$ $ $ $
Fourth Grade	
Fifth Grade	$ $ $ $ $

Each $ = $20.00

_____

Name _____ Date _____

Fill in the ◯ for the correct answer.

Use basic facts and patterns to find each product.

1. $3 \times 70 =$ 　(A) 180　　(B) 210　　(C) 240　　(D) 2,100

2. $6 \times 400 =$ 　(F) 240　　(G) 1,800　　(H) 2,400　　(J) 30,000

3. $8 \times 9,000 =$ 　(A) 7,000　　(B) 64,000　　(C) 72,000　　(D) 74,000

Find each product.

4. $\begin{array}{r} 43 \\ \times\ 6 \\ \hline \end{array}$ 　(F) 2,418　　(G) 258　　(H) 249　　(J) 198

5. $\begin{array}{r} 86 \\ \times\ 5 \\ \hline \end{array}$ 　(A) 430　　(B) 1,330　　(C) 4,011　　(D) 4,030

6. $\begin{array}{r} 72 \\ \times\ 9 \\ \hline \end{array}$ 　(F) 631　　(G) 638　　(H) 648　　(J) 711

7. $\begin{array}{r} 642 \\ \times\ 7 \\ \hline \end{array}$ 　(A) 44,814　　(B) 4,494　　(C) 4,484　　(D) 4,294

8. $3 \times \$8.46 =$ 　(F) \$24.38　　(G) \$25.38　　(H) \$26.01　　(J) \$252.18

9. $\begin{array}{r} 495 \\ \times\ 6 \\ \hline \end{array}$ 　(A) 2,470　　(B) 2,940　　(C) 2,970　　(D) 2,943

Name _____   Date _____

Find each product.

10.   3,894
          $\times$ 8

(F) 25,344   (G) 31,122   (H) 31,152   (J) 32,673

11. 2 $\times$ 4,663 =

(A) 12,116   (B) 9,326   (C) 8,326   (D) 6,885

12. 9 $\times$ 209 =

(F) 1,832   (G) 1,881   (H) 1,863   (J) 2,076

13. 4 $\times$ 3,008 =

(A) 12,032   (B) 12,083   (C) 12,122   (D) 12,422

14. 7 $\times$ 7,300 =

(F) 49,100   (G) 50,200   (H) 50,800   (J) 51,100

Estimate each product.

15.   65
          $\times$4

(A) 180   (B) 200   (C) 240   (D) 280

16.   788
          $\times$ 5

(F) 4,000   (G) 3,950   (H) 3,900   (J) 3,500

17.   3,289
          $\times$ 6

(A) 12,000   (B) 18,000   (C) 19,800   (D) 24,000

Multiply.

18.   40
          $\times$30

(F) 70   (G) 120   (H) 700   (J) 1,200

19.   800
          $\times$70

(A) 63,000   (B) 56,000   (C) 5,600   (D) 4,900

Name _____ Date _____

Multiply.

20.
$$\begin{array}{r} 36 \\ \times\, 24 \end{array}$$
(F) 210   (G) 216   (H) 864   (J) 882

21. $65 \times 83 =$ (A) 715   (B) 5,025   (C) 5,095   (D) 5,395

22. $489 \times 29 =$ (F) 5,379   (G) 13,758   (H) 14,181   (J) 20,881

23. Jon built 6 towers with blocks. The smallest was 4 blocks high, the next was 7 blocks high, and the third was 10 blocks high. If he continues this pattern, how many blocks high will the tallest tower be?

(A) 16   (B) 19   (C) 21   (D) 27

24. Bobby has a car collection. He has 24 cars displayed on each of 4 shelves. How many cars does he have in his collection?

(F) 6   (G) 20   (H) 28   (J) 96

25. The students at Oak Crest Elementary School raised money to donate to a local charity. If students in the fourth grade raised 3 times the amount of money students in the third grade raised, how much did the fourth grade raise?

Money Raised	
First Grade	$ $ $
Second Grade	$ $
Third Grade	$ $ $ $
Fourth Grade	
Fifth Grade	$ $ $ $ $

Each $ = $20.00

(A) $240   (B) $80   (C) $60   (D) $12

Name _____   Date _____

Do you remember?

1. $3 + 4 =$ _____

2. $8 + 2 =$ _____

3. $7 + 6 =$ _____

4. $9 + 8 =$ _____

5. $6 - 4 =$ _____

6. $11 - 5 =$ _____

7. $14 - 8 =$ _____

8. $16 - 9 =$ _____

9. $3 \times 7 =$ _____

10. $4 \times 8 =$ _____

11. $6 \times 7 =$ _____

12. $7 \times 8 =$ _____

13. $54 \div 9 =$ _____

14. $48 \div 6 =$ _____

15. $28 \div 7 =$ _____

16. $72 \div 8 =$ _____

17. $4\overline{)37}$

18. $7\overline{)24}$

19. $8\overline{)66}$

20. $6\overline{)34}$

Name _____ Date _____

Write all the factors of each number.

21. 12 _____

22. 15 _____

Try These!

Divide

23. 4)46

24. 2)44

25. 5)65

26. 7)99

27. 3)300

28. 5)5,000

29. 3)396

30. 5)606

31. 6)496

32. 8)656

33. 4)$0.72

34. 5)8.05

35. 2)413

36. 3)627

Name _____   Date _____

Write the correct answer.

Divide.

1. $4\overline{)44}$ _____

2. $4\overline{)35}$ _____

3. $6\overline{)83}$ _____

4. $6{,}400 \div 8 =$ _____

5. $143 \div 7 =$ _____

6. $8\overline{)\$7.60}$ _____

7. $4\overline{)160}$ _____

8. $520 \div 5 =$ _____

9. $5\overline{)605}$ _____

Estimate.

10. $29 \div 4 =$ _____   11. $48 \div 9 =$ _____

12. $219 \div 7 =$ _____   13. $553 \div 5 =$ _____

Divide.

14. $8\overline{)1{,}368}$ _____   15. $4\overline{)20{,}020}$ _____

16. $1{,}925 \div 5 =$ _____   17. $10{,}080 \div 8 =$ _____

Name _____ Date _____

18. Which numbers are divisible by 2, 5, and 10? _____

15, 20, 25, 35

19. Which number is prime? _____

4, 9, 15, 17

20. Which number is composite? _____

2, 4, 7, 19

21. Which list contains only prime numbers? _____

2, 5, 9, 12

2, 7, 17, 27

10, 15, 17, 19

11, 17, 19, 23

Find the average of the numbers in each group.

22. 63, 19, 17, 13 _____

23. 126, 134, 238 _____

24. Len is donating 28 pencils for his class supply box. If pencils are sold in packages of 8, how many packages does Len need to buy?

_____

25. Rosa sold 2 more candy bars than Ricky. Ricky sold 3 fewer candy bars than Rachael. Rachael sold twice as many candy bars as Rita. If Rita sold 15 candy bars, how many did Rosa sell?

_____

Name _____ Date _____

Fill in the ◯ for the correct answer.

Divide.

1. 4)44

   (A) 12   (B) 11   (C) 11   (D) 10

2. 4)35

   (F) 7 R7   (G) 8   (H) 8 R3   (J) 9

3. 6)83

   (A) 21   (B) 13 R5   (C) 13   (D) 12

4. 6,400 ÷ 8 =

   (F) 80   (G) 720   (H) 800   (J) 8,000

5. 143 ÷ 7 =

   (A) 20   (B) 20 R3   (C) 21 R3   (D) 23

6. 8)$7.60

   (F) $0.90   (G) $0.92   (H) $0.93   (J) $0.95

7. 4)160

   (A) 4   (B) 38   (C) 38 R8   (D) 40

8. 520 ÷ 5 =

   (F) 104   (G) 130   (H) 84   (J) 72

9. 5)605

   (A) 12 R5   (B) 120   (C) 120 R5   (D) 121

Name _____ Date _____

Estimate.

10. $29 \div 4 =$ ▨
(F) 5   (G) 6   (H) 7   (J) 8

11. $48 \div 9 =$ ▨
(A) 4   (B) 5   (C) 6   (D) 7

12. $219 \div 7 =$ ▨
(F) 20   (G) 30   (H) 35   (J) 40

13. $553 \div 5 =$ ▨
(A) 90   (B) 100   (C) 110   (D) 120

Divide.

14. $8\overline{)1,368}$
(F) 171   (G) 168   (H) 161   (J) 158

15. $4\overline{)20,020}$
(A) 4,005   (B) 5,000   (C) 5,004   (D) 5,005

16. $1,925 \div 5 =$ ▨
(F) 385   (G) 381   (H) 380   (J) 305

17. $10,080 \div 8 =$ ▨
(A) 1,210   (B) 1,259   (C) 1,260   (D) 1,261

18. Which number is divisible by 2, 5, and 10?

(F) 15   (G) 20   (H) 25   (J) all of these

19. Which number is prime?

(A) 17   (B) 15   (C) 9   (D) 4

Name _____ Date _____

20. Which number is composite?

(F) 19   (G) 7   (H) 4   (J) 2

21. Which list contains only prime numbers?

(A) 2, 5, 9, 12   (B) 2, 7, 17, 27   (C) 10, 15, 17, 19   (D) 11, 17, 19, 23

Find the average of the numbers in each group.

22. 63, 19, 17, 13

(F) 28   (G) 30   (H) 32   (J) 40

23. 126, 134, 238

(A) 125   (B) 166   (C) 249   (D) 498

24. Len is donating 28 pencils for his class supply box. If pencils are sold in packages of 8, how many packages does Len need to buy?

(F) 3   (G) 4   (H) 5   (J) 6

25. Rosa sold 2 more candy bars than Ricky. Ricky sold 3 fewer candy bars than Rachael. Rachael sold twice as many candy bars as Rita. If Rita sold 15 candy bars, how many did Rosa sell?

(A) 32   (B) 30   (C) 29   (D) 28

Name _____   Date _____

Do you remember?

Measure each line segment to the nearest inch or half inch.

1. ●————●   _____

2. ●———————————————●   _____

3. ●————————————●   _____

4. Measure to the nearest centimeter.

                                   _____

Answer each question about capacity.

5. Which unit would you use to measure the capacity of a water pitcher, cups or gallons?   _____

6. Which unit would you use to measure the capacity of a bathtub, pints or gallons?   _____

7. 1 liter = _____ milliliters

8. 3,000 milliliters = _____ liters

Answer each question about weight or mass.

9. Which unit would you use to measure the weight of a large dog, ounces or pounds?   _____

10. Which unit would you use to measure the mass of a box of cereal, grams or kilograms?   _____

11. 1 kilogram = _____ grams

12. 4,000 grams = _____ kilograms

Name _____ Date _____

What time is shown?

13.

_____

14.

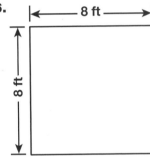

_____

Try These!

Find the perimeter of each figure.

15.

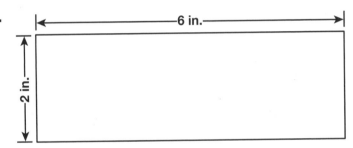

_____

16.

|← 8 ft →|
8 ft

_____

17.

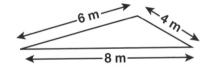

_____

18.

|← 5 cm →|
2 cm

_____

Find each missing number.

19. 3 yards = _____ feet

20. 6 feet = _____ inches

21. _____ gallons = 16 quarts

22. 32 ounces = _____ pounds

23. 5 meters = _____ centimeters

24. 3 kilometers = _____ meters

25. 6 liters = _____ milliliters

26. _____ kilograms = 3,000 grams

Name _____ Date _____

Write each temperature.

27.

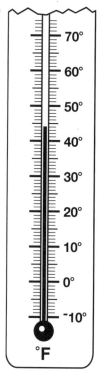

_____

28.

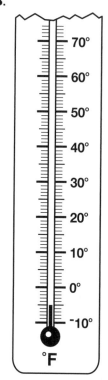

_____

29.

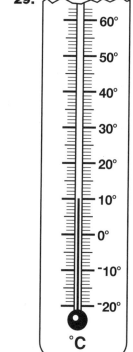

_____

30.

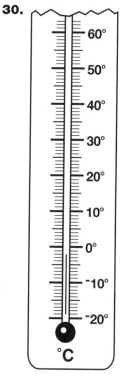

_____

Name _____ Date _____

Write the correct answer.

Find the perimeter of each figure.

1.

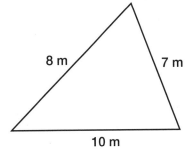

10 ft

5 ft   5 ft

10 ft

_____

2.

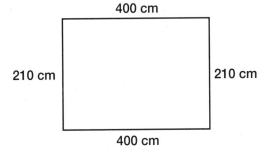

8 m   7 m

10 m

_____

3.

400 cm

210 cm   210 cm

400 cm

_____

Write each missing number.

4. 4 miles = _____ yards

5. 30 decimeters = _____ meters

6. 36 inches = _____ feet

7. 8 quarts = _____ gallons

8. _____ pounds = 6 tons

9. 4 liters = _____ milliliters

10. 10,000 grams = _____ kilograms

Name _____ Date _____

Compare. Write >, < , *or* = in each ◯.

11. 24 feet ◯ 8 yards

12. 24 inches ◯ 1 yard

13. 4,000 meters ◯ 2 kilometers

14. 8 cups ◯ 2 pints

Choose the most appropriate unit of measure.

15. width of a table _____

16. mass of a car _____

Find each temperature.

17.
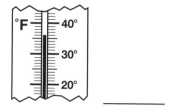
_____

18.
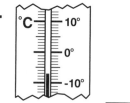
_____

19. On Monday, the high temperature in New York City was 14°F cooler than the high temperature in Chicago. If the high temperature in Chicago on Monday was 70°F, what was the high temperature in New York on Monday?

_____

20. Billie built a rectangular swimming pool in her backyard. If one side of the pool is 10 feet long, what is the perimeter?

_____

Name _____ Date _____

Find the perimeter of each figure.

1.

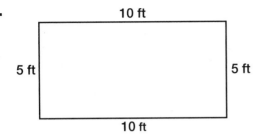

(A) 15 ft   (B) 30 ft

(C) 25 ft   (D) 50 ft

2.

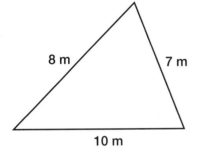

(F) 25 m   (G) 280 m

(H) 30 m   (J) 560 m

3.

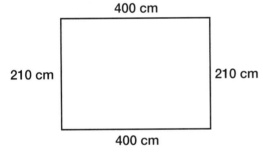

(A) 84,000 cm   (B) 1,210 cm

(C) 1,220 cm   (D) 610 cm

Find each missing number.

4. 4 miles = _____ yards   (F) 440   (G) 7,000   (H) 7,040   (J) 21.120

5. 30 decimeters = _____ meters   (A) 300   (B) 10   (C) 6   (D) 3

6. 36 inches = _____ feet   (F) 3   (G) 9   (H) 12   (J) 15

7. 8 quarts = _____ gallons   (A) 1   (B) 2   (C) 4   (D) 8

Name _____ Date _____

Find each missing number.

8. _____ pounds = 6 tons

(F) 18,000   (G) 12,000   (H) 6,000   (J) 1,200

9. 4 liters = _____ milliliters

(A) 40   (B) 400   (C) 4,000   (D) 8,000

10. 10,000 grams = _____ kilograms

(F) 1   (G) 10   (H) 20   (J) 100

Which symbol makes each statement true?

11. 24 feet ⬤ 8 yards

(A) >   (B) <

(C) =   (D) +

12. 24 inches ⬤ 1 yard

(F) >   (G) <

(H) =   (J) +

13. 4,000 meters ⬤ 2 kilometers

(A) >   (B) <

(C) =   (D) +

14. 8 cups 2 pints

(F) >   (G) <

(H) =   (J) +

Choose the most appropriate unit of measure.

15. width of a table

(A) inches   (B) feet

(C) yards   (D) miles

16. mass of a car

(F) kilograms   (G) milligrams

(H) grams   (J) ounces

Name _____   Date _____

Find each temperature.

17.
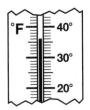

(A) ⁻36°F   (B) ⁻35°F

(C) 36°F   (D) 37°F

18.
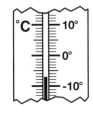

(F) ⁻7°C   (G) ⁻6°C

(H) 6°C   (J) 7°C

19. On Monday, the high temperature in New York City was 14°F cooler than the high temperature in Chicago. If the high temperature in Chicago on Monday was 70°F, what was the high temperature in New York on Monday?

(A) 50°F   (B) 56°F

(C) 84°F   (D) 90°F

20. Billie built a rectangular swimming pool in her backyard. If one side of the pool is 10 feet long, what is the perimeter?

(F) 100 ft   (G) 40 ft

(H) 20 ft   (J) not enough information

Name _____ Date _____

Do you remember?

Write a fraction for the shaded part.

1. 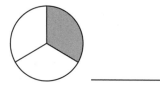 _____

2. 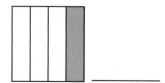 _____

Write a fraction for the shaded part.

3. _____

4.  _____

Compare. Write >, <, or = in each ◯.

5. $\frac{1}{2}$ ◯ $\frac{1}{3}$

6. $\frac{1}{8}$ ◯ $\frac{1}{8}$

7. $\frac{1}{9}$ ◯ $\frac{1}{4}$

8. $\frac{1}{5}$ ◯ $\frac{1}{6}$

Write *yes* or *no* to tell whether each pair of fractions is equivalent.

9. $\frac{2}{3}$ and $\frac{4}{6}$ _____

10. $\frac{1}{4}$ and $\frac{3}{8}$ _____

11. $\frac{3}{5}$ and $\frac{6}{10}$ _____

12. $\frac{5}{6}$ and $\frac{1}{3}$ _____

Try These!

Write the fraction for the shaded part.

13. 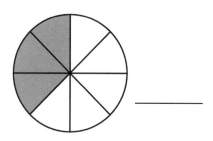 _____

14. _____

Name _____ Date _____

Find the fractional part of each number.

15. $\frac{1}{3}$ of 9 _____

16. $\frac{1}{2}$ of 16 _____

17. $\frac{3}{4}$ of 8 _____

18. $\frac{2}{3}$ of 12 _____

Write each fraction in simplest form.

19. $\frac{9}{12}$ _____

20. $\frac{10}{15}$ _____

Compare. Write >, <, or = in each $\bigcirc$.

21. $\frac{4}{9}$ $\bigcirc$ $\frac{2}{9}$

22. $\frac{2}{3}$ $\bigcirc$ $\frac{5}{6}$

23. Write a mixed number for $\frac{8}{3}$. _____

24. Write an improper fraction for $3\frac{3}{4}$. _____

Add or subtract. Write each sum or difference in simplest form.

25. $\frac{4}{6} + \frac{1}{6}$ _____

26. $\frac{5}{9} + \frac{3}{9}$ _____

27. $2\frac{3}{7} + 4\frac{3}{7}$ _____

28. $4\frac{1}{3} + 3\frac{2}{3}$ _____

29. $\frac{9}{10} - \frac{5}{10}$ _____

30. $\frac{4}{5} - \frac{2}{5}$ _____

31. $8\frac{3}{4} - 6\frac{3}{4}$ _____

32. $7\frac{4}{7} - 2\frac{3}{7}$ _____

Name _____ Date _____

Write the correct answer.

1. Write the fraction for the shaded part.

 _____

Find the fractional part of each number.

2. $\frac{2}{3}$ of 9   _____

3. $\frac{2}{5}$ of 10   _____

Write the mixed number or whole number for each improper fraction.

4. $\frac{13}{5}$ _____

5. $\frac{15}{3}$ _____

Write the improper fraction for each mixed number.

6. $3\frac{4}{5}$ _____

7. $2\frac{3}{4}$ _____

8. $2\frac{3}{5}$ _____

Write each fraction in simplest form.

9. $\frac{12}{15}$ _____

10. $\frac{10}{16}$ _____

11. Which fraction is in simplest form?   _____

$\frac{3}{9}$ $\frac{4}{12}$ $\frac{2}{3}$ $\frac{8}{10}$

12. Which fraction is not in simplest form?   _____

$\frac{5}{15}$ $\frac{5}{12}$ $\frac{5}{9}$ $\frac{5}{8}$

Name _____ Date _____

13. Multiply or divide to find the equivalent fraction.

$$\frac{2}{4} = \frac{2 \times 4}{4 \times \square} = \frac{\square}{\square}$$

Compare. Write $>, <,$ *or* $=$.

14. $\frac{9}{16} \bigcirc \frac{5}{16}$

15. $\frac{12}{5} \bigcirc \frac{24}{10}$

Add or subtract. Write the sum or difference in simplest form.

16. $\frac{3}{9} + \frac{4}{9} =$ _____

17. $\frac{2}{10} + \frac{6}{10} =$ _____

18. $2\frac{3}{5} + 3\frac{2}{5} =$ _____

19. $4\frac{1}{6} + 3\frac{1}{6} =$ _____

20. $\frac{7}{8} - \frac{3}{8} =$ _____

21. $\frac{4}{5} - \frac{1}{5} =$ _____

22. $8\frac{7}{9} - 7\frac{6}{9} =$ _____

23. $2\frac{7}{8} - 1\frac{4}{8} =$ _____

24. There are 18 players on Coach Allen's baseball team. Three players were injured in a game last week. What fraction of the players were not injured? Write the answer in simplest form.

_____

25. Suzie's grandmother made two pizzas. She cut each pizza into 8 pieces. After Suzie and three of her friends ate the pizzas, there was 1 piece of each left. Which mixed number describes the part of the two whole pizzas Suzie and her friends ate?

_____

Name _____   Date _____

Fill in the ◯ for the correct answer.

1. Write the fraction for the shaded part.

   (A) $\frac{3}{5}$ (B) $\frac{2}{5}$ (C) $\frac{3}{10}$ (D) $\frac{2}{10}$

Find the fractional part of each number.

2. $\frac{2}{3}$ of 9   (F) 3   (G) 4   (H) 6   (J) 9

3. $\frac{2}{5}$ of 10   (A) 9   (B) 6   (C) 5   (D) 4

Write the mixed number or whole number for each improper fraction.

4. $\frac{13}{5}$ (F) $2\frac{5}{3}$ (G) $2\frac{3}{5}$ (H) $2\frac{1}{5}$ (J) $1\frac{3}{5}$

5. $\frac{15}{3}$ (A) $3\frac{3}{5}$ (B) $4\frac{1}{3}$ (C) $4\frac{2}{3}$ (D) 5

Write the improper fraction for each mixed number.

6. $3\frac{4}{5}$ (F) 19   (G) $\frac{23}{5}$ (H) $\frac{19}{5}$ (J) $\frac{17}{5}$

7. $2\frac{3}{4}$ (A) $\frac{10}{4}$ (B) $\frac{11}{4}$ (C) $\frac{14}{4}$ (D) 11

8. $2\frac{3}{5}$ (F) $\frac{10}{5}$ (G) $\frac{11}{5}$ (H) $\frac{13}{5}$ (J) 14

Write each fraction in simplest form.

9. $\frac{12}{15}$ (A) $\frac{5}{6}$ (B) $\frac{4}{5}$ (C) $\frac{2}{3}$ (D) $\frac{3}{5}$

10. $\frac{10}{16}$ (F) $\frac{5}{8}$ (G) $\frac{4}{10}$ (H) $\frac{2}{5}$ (J) $\frac{3}{8}$

Name _____ Date _____

11. Which fraction is in simplest form?

(A) $\frac{3}{9}$ (B) $\frac{4}{12}$ (C) $\frac{2}{3}$ (D) $\frac{8}{10}$

12. Which fraction is not in simplest form?

(F) $\frac{5}{15}$ (G) $\frac{5}{12}$ (H) $\frac{5}{9}$ (J) $\frac{5}{8}$

13. Multiply or divide to find the equivalent fraction.

$$\frac{2}{4} = \frac{2 \times 4}{4 \times \boxed{}} = \frac{\boxed{}}{\boxed{}}$$

(A) 4, 8, 16 (B) 2, 4, 8 (C) 4, 8, 12 (D) 4, 4, 16

Which symbol makes each statement true?

14. $\frac{9}{16}$ ▨ $\frac{5}{16}$

(F) > (G) < (H) = (J) +

15. $\frac{12}{5}$ ▨ $\frac{24}{10}$

(A) > (B) < (C) = (D) +

Add or subtract. Write the sum or difference in simplest form.

16. $\frac{3}{9} + \frac{4}{9} =$

(F) 9 (G) $\frac{12}{9}$ (H) $\frac{7}{9}$ (J) $\frac{1}{9}$

17. $\frac{2}{10} + \frac{6}{10} =$

(A) $\frac{12}{10}$ (B) $\frac{8}{10}$ (C) $\frac{4}{5}$ (D) $\frac{4}{10}$

18. $2\frac{3}{5} + 3\frac{2}{5} =$

(F) 9 (G) $8\frac{3}{5}$ (H) $8\frac{2}{5}$ (J) $8\frac{1}{5}$

19. $4\frac{1}{6} + 3\frac{1}{6} =$

(A) $7\frac{2}{3}$ (B) $7\frac{4}{6}$ (C) $7\frac{4}{12}$ (D) $7\frac{1}{3}$

20. $\frac{7}{8} - \frac{3}{8} =$

(F) $1\frac{1}{4}$ (G) $\frac{10}{8}$ (H) $\frac{4}{8}$ (J) $\frac{1}{2}$

21. $\frac{4}{5} - \frac{1}{5} =$

(A) 1 (B) $\frac{3}{5}$ (C) $\frac{2}{5}$ (D) $\frac{1}{5}$

Name _____ Date _____

22. $8\frac{7}{9} - 7\frac{6}{9} =$

    (F) $12\frac{4}{9}$ (G) $1\frac{1}{9}$

    (H) $\frac{10}{9}$ (J) $\frac{1}{9}$

---

23. $2\frac{7}{8} - 1\frac{4}{8} =$

    (A) $2\frac{3}{8}$ (B) $1\frac{3}{8}$

    (C) $1\frac{1}{8}$ (D) $\frac{3}{8}$

---

24. There are 18 players on Coach Allen's baseball team. Three players were injured in a game last week. What fraction of the players were not injured? Write the answer in simplest form.

    (F) $\frac{3}{18}$ (G) $\frac{3}{15}$

    (H) $\frac{5}{6}$ (J) $5\frac{3}{18}$

---

25. Suzie's grandmother made two pizzas. She cut each pizza into 8 pieces. After Suzie and three of her friends ate the pizzas, there was 1 piece of each left. Which mixed number describes the part of the two whole pizzas Suzie and her friends ate?

    (A) $1\frac{7}{8}$ (B) $1\frac{2}{3}$

    (C) $1\frac{1}{2}$ (D) $1\frac{7}{8}$

Name _____   Date _____

Do you remember?

Write each fraction as a decimal.

1. $\frac{2}{10}$ _____

2. $\frac{9}{10}$ _____

3. $\frac{15}{100}$ _____

4. $\frac{7}{100}$ _____

Write a decimal for each shaded part.

5.  _____

6. _____

7.  _____

8. 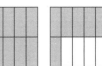 _____

Write a decimal for each shaded part.

9. _____

10. 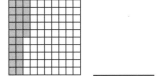 _____

11. 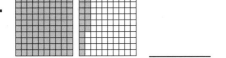 _____

12. 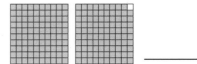 _____

Try These!

Write each mixed number as a decimal.

13. $4\frac{3}{10}$ _____

14. $35\frac{6}{100}$ _____

Name _____ Date _____

Write a fraction and a decimal to describe each model.

15.  _____

16. 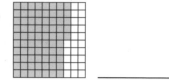 _____

Compare. Write >, <, or = in each ◯.

17. 8.6 ◯ 6.8

18. 4.2 ◯ 4.20

19. 5.13 ◯ 5.31

20. 6.04 ◯ 6.40

Write the numbers in order from least to greatest.

21. $2\frac{1}{10}$ 2.4   2.04   _____

22. $15\frac{17}{100}$ 15.1   15.7   _____

Add or subtract.

23. $\begin{array}{r} 0.23 \\ +\,0.15 \\ \hline \end{array}$

24. $\begin{array}{r} 2.7 \\ +\,3.1 \\ \hline \end{array}$

25. $\begin{array}{r} 46.2 \\ -\,4.7 \\ \hline \end{array}$

26. $\begin{array}{r} 184.2 \\ -\,85.7 \\ \hline \end{array}$

Round each decimal to the nearest whole number.

27. 4.45   _____

28. 18.73   _____

Round each decimal to the nearest tenth.

29. 16.59   _____

30. 9.23   _____

Estimate each sum or difference. Round to the nearest whole number.

31. $\begin{array}{r} 6.8 \\ +\,3.2 \\ \hline \end{array}$

32. $\begin{array}{r} 14.6 \\ +\,2.4 \\ \hline \end{array}$

33. $\begin{array}{r} 26.9 \\ -\,14.6 \\ \hline \end{array}$

34. $\begin{array}{r} 226.4 \\ -\,113.7 \\ \hline \end{array}$

Name _____ Date _____

Write the correct answer.

Write each mixed number as a decimal.

1. $4\frac{30}{100}$ _____

2. $2\frac{6}{10}$ _____

3. $31\frac{50}{100}$ _____

4. Write the correct decimal for the following amount.

one and forty-two hundredths _____

Write a mixed number for the following amount.

5. one and forty-two hundredths _____

Compare. Write >, <, or =.

6. 4.1 $\bigcirc$ 4.11

7. 7.50 $\bigcirc$ 7.5

8. 0.2 $\bigcirc$ $\frac{2}{100}$

9. 3.26 $\bigcirc$ $3\frac{26}{100}$

10. Order from least to greatest.

1    $2\frac{1}{2}$ 2.25   2

_____

11. Order from greatest to least.

$12\frac{2}{100}$ 12.04   12.4 $12\frac{2}{10}$

_____

Name _____ Date _____

Add or subtract.

12.　5.6
　　　+ 2.8

13.　12.23
　　　+ 8.82

14.　135.06
　　　+ 237.95

15.　17.7
　　　− 9.2

16.　26.04
　　　− 19.22

17. Round 25.7 to the nearest whole number. _____

18. Round 16.85 to the nearest tenth. _____

**Estimate each sum or difference. Round to the
nearest whole number.**

19.　6.8
　　　+ 7.2

20.　172.7
　　　+ 135.2

21.　24.2
　　　− 18.8

22.　245.1
　　　− 121.7

23. Janie earns $4.00 babysitting. She saves $2.15 of her earnings and spends the rest. How much does she spend?

_____

24. Jim is buying a package of sliced turkey for $3.49. If Jim
has $10, how much money will he have left after buying
the turkey?

_____

25. Beth's basketball team is raising money. The first week,
Beth and her teammates raised $10. The second week,
they raised $20. The third week, they raised $30. If the
pattern continued, during which week will they raise $80?

_____

Name _____ Date _____

Fill in the ◯ for the correct answer.

Choose the correct decimal for each mixed number.

1. $4\frac{30}{100}$

　　Ⓐ 4.03　　　　Ⓑ 4.30　　　　Ⓒ 43.0　　　　Ⓓ 430.0

2. $2\frac{6}{10}$

　　Ⓕ 261.0　　　Ⓖ 26.0　　　Ⓗ 2.6　　　Ⓙ 0.26

3. $31\frac{50}{100}$

　　Ⓐ 3.15　　　Ⓑ 31.50　　　Ⓒ 315.0　　　Ⓓ 31,500.0

4. Choose the correct decimal for the following amount.
one and forty-two hundredths

　　Ⓕ 142.0　　　Ⓖ 4.2

　　Ⓗ 1.42　　　Ⓙ 0.142

5. Choose the correct mixed number for the following amount.
one and forty-two hundredths

　　Ⓐ $\frac{142}{1,000}$　　　Ⓑ $14\frac{2}{10}$

　　Ⓒ $\frac{142}{100}$　　　Ⓓ $1\frac{42}{100}$

Which symbol makes each statement true?

6. 4.1 4.11

　　Ⓕ >　　　Ⓖ <　　　Ⓗ =　　　Ⓙ +

7. 7.50 7.5

　　Ⓐ >　　　Ⓑ <　　　Ⓒ =　　　Ⓓ +

Name _____ Date _____

8. 0.2 ◯ $\frac{2}{100}$

    (F) >   (G) <   (H) =   (J) +

9. 3.26 ◯ $3\frac{26}{100}$

    (A) >   (B) <   (C) =   (D) +

10. Order from least to greatest.

1    $2\frac{1}{2}$ 2.25   2

(F) 1	2	$2\frac{1}{2}$	2.25
(G) 1	2	2.25	$2\frac{1}{2}$
(H) 2.25	$2\frac{1}{2}$	2	1
(J) $2\frac{1}{2}$	2.25	2	1

11. Order from greatest to least.

$12\frac{2}{100}$ 12.04   12.4 $12\frac{2}{10}$

(A) 12.04	12.4	$12\frac{2}{100}$	$12\frac{2}{10}$
(B) 12.04	$12\frac{2}{100}$	12.4	$12\frac{2}{10}$
(C) 12.4	$12\frac{2}{100}$	12.04	$12\frac{2}{10}$
(D) 12.4	$12\frac{2}{10}$	12.04	$12\frac{2}{100}$

Name _____ Date _____

Add or subtract.

12. 5.6
   $+\,2.8$

(F) 8.4   (G) 8.2   (H) 7.4   (J) 7.2

13. 12.23
   $+\,8.82$

(A) 20.05   (B) 20.5   (C) 21.05   (D) 21.5

14. 135.06
   $+\,237.95$

(F) 362.01   (G) 362.91   (H) 372.01   (J) 373.01

15. 17.7
   $-\,9.2$

(A) 12.5   (B) 8.5   (C) 7.5   (D) 2.5

16. 26.04
   $-\,19.22$

(F) 16.82   (G) 13.82   (H) 6.82   (J) 3.72

17. Round 25.7 to the nearest whole number.

(A) 2,570   (B) 257   (C) 26   (D) 25

18. Round 16.85 to the nearest tenth.

(F) 16.9   (G) 168.5   (H) 169.0   (J) 1,685.0

Name _____ Date _____

Estimate each sum or difference. Round to the nearest whole number.

19. 6.8
      $+ 7.2$

(A) 12 (B) 13 (C) 14 (D) 15

20. 172.7
       $+ 135.2$

(F) 37.5 (G) 307.9 (H) 308 (J) 400

21. 24.2
       $- 18.8$

(A) 5 (B) 6 (C) 44 (D) 45

22. 245.1
       $- 121.7$

(F) 366.8 (G) 123.4 (H) 124 (J) 123

23. Janie earns $4.00 babysitting. She saves $\frac{3}{5}$ of her earnings and spends the rest. How much does she spend?

(A) $5.60 (B) $3.65 (C) $0.35 (D) $1.60

24. Jim is buying a package of sliced turkey for $3.49. If Jim has $10, how much money will he have left after buying the turkey?

(F) $7.51 (G) $6.51 (H) $4.39 (J) $3.39

25. Beth's basketball team is raising money. The first week, Beth and her team-mates raised $10. The second week, they raised $20. The third week, they raised $30. If the pattern continued, during which week will they raise $80?

(A) fifth (B) sixth (C) seventh (D) eighth

Name _____ Date _____

Do you remember?

1. Twenty-five first grade students chose their favorite flavor of ice cream from the following choices: vanilla, chocolate, strawberry, and peach. Fifteen students chose vanilla, one chose chocolate, six chose strawberry, and three chose peach. Make a tally chart to organize this information.

Flavor	Tally	Number
Vanilla		
Chocolate		
Strawberry		
Peach		

Kendra collects stuffed animals. The following bar graph shows how many of each type of stuffed animal she has.

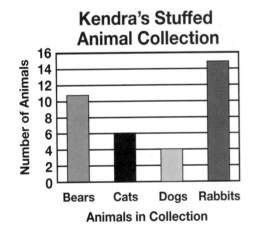

2. How many stuffed rabbits does Kendra have?

   _____

3. Which stuffed animal does she have the least of?

   _____

4. You put 5 yellow blocks, 9 blue blocks, and 2 green blocks in a sack and choose one without looking. How would you describe the probability of choosing a blue block? Write *certain*, *likely*, *unlikely*, or *impossible*.

   _____

Name _____ Date _____

Try These!

Find the range, mode, median, and mean.

5. 3, 5, 3, 9

_____

6. 10, 15, 5, 15, 20

_____

Use the graph below for Questions 7 and 8.

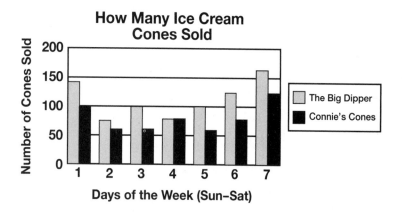

7. Which store sold the most ice cream for the week?

_____

8. Would you expect sales to be up or down the next day?

_____

Name _____   Date _____

Use the graph below for Questions 9 and 10.

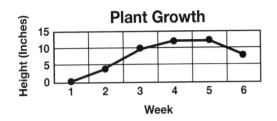

9. Which week did the plant grow the most?

_____

10. How much did the plant grow during the week?

_____

Use the spinners for Questions 11–14.

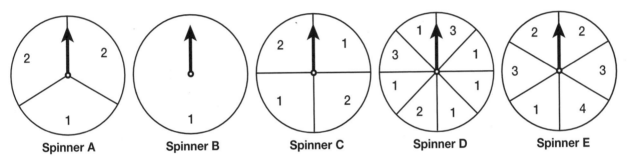

11. On which spinner would you be equally likely to spin 1 or 2?

_____

12. You spin Spinner E once. Write a fraction to describe the probability that the spinner lands on 1.

_____

13. You spin Spinner D 12 times. How many times is the spinner likely to land on 3?

_____

14. Use a tree diagram. You spin Spinner A once and Spinner E once. What is the probability that both spinners will land on 2?

_____

Name _____ Date _____

Write the correct answer.

Find the range, mode, median, and mean. Then identify any outliers.

1. 4, 10, 6, 4 _____

2. 40, 50, 45, 90, 45

_____

Use the graph for Questions 3–6.

3. In which month was the difference between the number of books read by fourth graders and fifth graders the greatest?

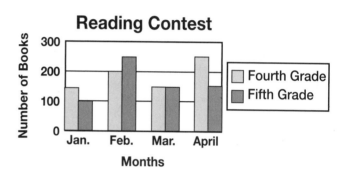

_____

4. In which month did the fourth and fifth graders read the same number of books?

_____

5. Who read more books in all, the fourth graders or fifth graders? How many more did they read?

_____

6. There are 50 fourth graders. What is the mean of the of books read by fourth graders in January?

_____

Use the graph for Questions 7–10.

7. Between which two times did the temperature change the most?

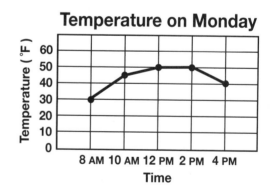

_____

8. At what time was the temperature 45°F?

_____

9. Between which two times did the temperature stay the same?

_____

10. How many degrees did the temperature decrease from 2 PM to 4 PM?

_____

Name _____ Date _____

A bag contains 1 green marble, 3 red marbles, and 4 yellow marbles. Write *certain*, *likely*, *unlikely*, or *impossible* for Questions 11–13.

11. What is the probability of choosing a green marble from the bag? _____

12. What is the probability of choosing a blue marble from the bag? _____

13. What is the probability of choosing a yellow marble from the bag? _____

Use the spinner below for Questions 14–16. Write the correct answer.

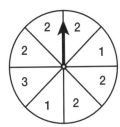

14. What is the probability of spinning a "3"? _____

15. What is the probability of spinning a "2"? _____

16. What is the probability of spinning a "1"? _____

You write each of the letters P, R, O, B, A, B, I, L, I, T, Y on a card and place the cards in a bag.

17. If you pick a card without looking, which two letters are you most likely to pick? _____

18. If you pick a card and put it back 44 times, how many times would you probably pick the letter "T"? _____

19. Bryan and Kyle live on Oak Street. Kyle lives 8 blocks from Lion's Park and Bryan lives 3 blocks on the other side of Lion's Park. If Kyle rides his bike to Bryan's house and back home, how many blocks does he ride on the round trip? _____

20. You spin Spinner A and then spin Spinner B. If you do this 32 times, how many times will you probably spin a 3 on both spinners?

_____

Spinner A

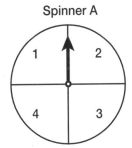

Spinner B

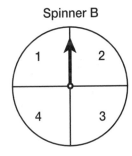

Name _____ Date _____

Fill in the ◯ for the correct answer.

Find the range, mode, median, and mean. Then identify any outliers.

1. 4, 10, 6, 4

- **A** range = 6
  mode = 4
  median = 5
  mean = 6
  no outliers

- **B** range = 6
  mode = 4
  median = 6
  mean = 6
  no outliers

- **C** range = 6
  mode = 4
  median = 5
  mean = 6
  outlier = 10

- **D** range = 6
  mode = 4
  median = 8
  mean = 6
  outlier = 10

2. 40, 50, 45, 90, 45

- **F** range = 50
  mode = 45
  median = 50
  mean = 54
  outlier = 90

- **G** range = 50
  mode = 45
  median = 45
  mean = 54
  outlier = 90

- **H** range = 50
  mode = 45
  median = 45
  mean = 54
  no outliers

- **J** range = 50
  mode = 45
  median = 50
  mean = 54
  no outliers

Use the graph for Questions 3–5.

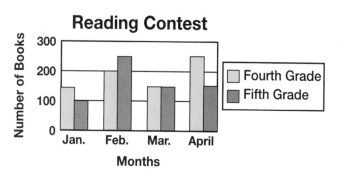

Reading Contest

3. In which month was the difference between the number of books read by fourth graders and fifth graders the greatest?

- **A** January
- **B** February
- **C** March
- **D** April

4. In which month did the fourth and fifth graders read the same number of books?

- **F** January
- **G** February
- **H** March
- **J** April

5. Who read more books in all, the fourth graders or fifth graders? How many more did they read?

- **A** fourth; 100
- **B** fourth; 250
- **C** fifth; 100
- **D** fifth; 250

Name _____ Date _____

6. There are 50 fourth graders. What is the mean of the number of books read by fourth graders in January?

(A) 150　　　(B) 50　　　(C) 15　　　(D) 3

Use the graph for Questions 7-10.

7. Between which two times did the temperature change the most?

(F) 8 AM to 10 AM　　(G) 10 AM to 12 PM

(H) 12 PM to 2 PM　　(J) 2 PM to 4 PM

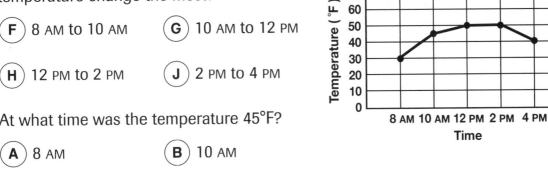

Temperature on Monday

8. At what time was the temperature 45°F?

(A) 8 AM　　　　(B) 10 AM

(C) 12 PM　　　　(D) 4 PM

9. Between which two times did the temperature stay the same?

(F) 8 AM to 10 AM　　(G) 10 AM to 12 PM

(H) 12 PM to 2 PM　　(J) 2 PM to 4 PM

10. How many degrees did the temperature decrease from 2 PM to 4 PM?

(A) 2　　　　(B) 5

(C) 10　　　　(D) 20

Name _____ Date _____

A bag contains 1 green marble, 3 red marbles, and 4 yellow marbles. Choose *certain*, *likely*, *unlikely*, or *impossible* for Questions 11-13.

11. What is the probability of choosing a green marble from the bag?

(**A**) certain   (**B**) likely

(**C**) unlikely   (**D**) impossible

12. What is the probability of choosing a blue marble from the bag?

(**F**) certain   (**G**) likely

(**H**) unlikely   (**J**) impossible

13. What is the probability of choosing a yellow marble from the bag?

(**A**) certain   (**B**) likely

(**C**) unlikely   (**D**) impossible

Use the spinner below for Questions 14-16.

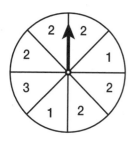

14. What is the probability of spinning a "3"?

(**F**) $\dfrac{1}{8}$ (**G**) $\dfrac{3}{12}$ (**H**) $\dfrac{3}{8}$ (**J**) $\dfrac{3}{7}$

15. What is the probability of spinning a "2"?

(**A**) $\dfrac{1}{8}$ (**B**) $\dfrac{3}{8}$ (**C**) $\dfrac{6}{8}$ (**D**) $\dfrac{5}{8}$

16. What is the probability of spinning a "1"?

(**F**) $\dfrac{1}{8}$ (**G**) $\dfrac{1}{4}$ (**H**) $\dfrac{1}{2}$ (**J**) $\dfrac{6}{8}$

Name _____ Date _____

You write each of the letters P, R, O, B, A, B, I, L, I, T, and Y on a card and place the cards in a bag.

17. If you pick a card without looking, which two letters are you most likely to pick?

(A) P and Y   (B) L and O   (C) B and I   (D) A and R

---

18. If you pick a card and put it back 44 times, how many times would you probably pick the letter "T"?

(F) 22   (G) 11   (H) 10   (J) 4

---

19. Bryan and Kyle live on Oak Street. Kyle lives 8 blocks from Lion's Park and Bryan lives 3 blocks on the other side of Lion's Park. If Kyle rides his bike to Bryan's house and back home, how many blocks does he ride on the round trip?

(A) 5   (B) 11   (C) 22   (D) 24

---

20. Spin Spinner A and then spin Spinner B. If you do this 32 times, how many times will you probably spin a 3 on both spinners?

(F) 2   (G) 4   (H) 6   (J) 8

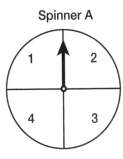

Spinner A

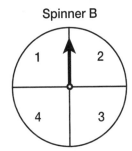

Spinner B

Name _____   Date _____

Do you remember?

Name each figure.

1. 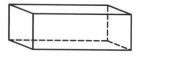 _____

2. 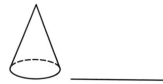 _____

Name each solid figure.

3.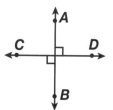

_____

4. 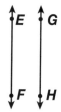 _____

Draw the other half of each figure.

5.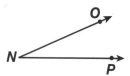

6.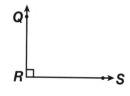

Try These!

Write *parallel, intersecting,* or *perpendicular* to describe the relationship between each pair of lines.

7.

_____

8.

_____

Write *acute, right,* or *obtuse* to describe each angle.

9.

_____

10.

_____

Name _____   Date _____

11. Name the quadrilateral with the most specific name possible.

_____

12. Name the triangle by both its angles and its sides.

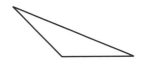

_____

13. Name the part of the circle shown by the segment in the figure below.

_____

14. Are the two figures congruent? Write yes or no.

_____

Write *line symmetry*, *rotational symmetry*, or *no symmetry* to describe each figure.

15.

_____

16.

_____

Use the figure below for Questions 17 and 18.

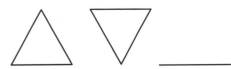

17. Find the perimeter. _____

18. Find the area. _____

19. Name the solid figure that can be made with the following net.

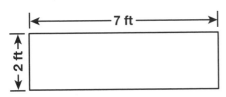

_____

Use the figure below for Questions 20 and 21.

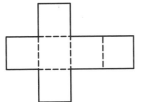

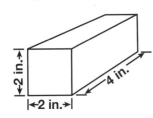

20. Find the surface area. _____

21. Find the volume. _____

Name _____ Date _____

Write the correct answer.

Write *parallel*, *intersecting*, or *perpendicular* to describe the relationship between each pair of lines.

1.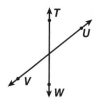

2.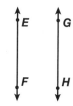

3.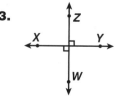

_____   _____   _____

Name each figure.

4.

_____

5.

_____

6.

_____

7.

_____

Name the solid figure that could be made with each net.

8.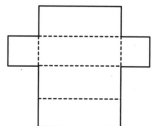

9.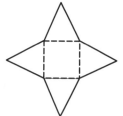

_____   _____

Name _____ Date _____

Write the correct answer.

10. Which figure is congruent to the first figure?

  a. **b.** **c.** **d.**

11. How many lines of symmetry does the following figure have?

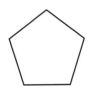 _____

Find the perimeter of each figure.

12. |← 4 ft →|
4 ft
_____

13. |← 8 m →|
2 m
_____

14. |← 5 in. →|
2 in.
_____

15.
1 cm
1 cm
1 cm
|← 4 cm →|
_____

Find the area of each figure.

16. |← 5 m →|
5 m
_____

17. |← 6 in. →|
4 in.
_____

18.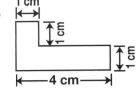
1 cm
1 cm
1 cm
|← 4 cm →|
_____

19. What is the volume of a rectangular prism that is 3 ft long, 2 ft high, and 4 ft long?

_____

20. What two different shapes could be used to form a figure congruent to the one below?

_____

Name _____ Date _____

Fill in the ◯ for the correct answer.

Choose the term that describes the relationship between each pair of lines.

1.
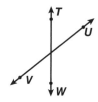

- (A) parallel
- (B) intersecting
- (C) perpendicular
- (D) line segment

2.
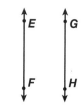

- (F) parallel
- (G) intersecting
- (H) perpendicular
- (J) line segment

3.
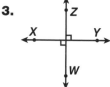

- (A) parallel
- (B) intersecting
- (C) perpendicular
- (D) line segment

Choose the correct name for each figure.

4.

- (F) triangle
- (H) pentagon
- (G) trapezoid
- (J) parallelogram

5.

- (A) triangle
- (C) trapezoid
- (B) pentagon
- (D) parallelogram

6.

- (F) obtuse, scalene triangle
- (H) obtuse, isosceles triangle
- (G) acute, scalene triangle
- (J) obtuse, isosceles triangle

7.

- (A) right triangle
- (C) scalene triangle
- (B) obtuse triangle
- (D) isosceles triangle

Name _____   Date _____

Fill in the ◯ for the correct answer.

Name the solid figure that could be made with each net.

8.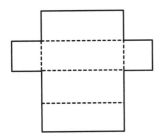

    (F) triangular pyramid   (G) rectangular prism

    (H) rectangle   (J) cube

9.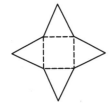

    (A) cube   (B) rectangular prism

    (C) square pyramid   (D) triangular prism

10. Which figure is congruent to the figure below?

    (F)   (G)

    (H)   (J)

11. How many lines of symmetry does the following figure have?

    (A) one   (B) two

    (C) three   (D) five

Find the perimeter of each figure.

12.

    (F) 16 ft   (G) 12 ft

    (H) 8 ft   (J) 4 ft

Name _____ Date _____

Fill in the ◯ for the correct answer.

13. |←——8 m——→| 2 m

       A 10 m   **B** 16 m

       C 20 m   **D** 24 m

14. |←—— 5 in. ——→| 2 in.

       F 14 in.   **G** 10 in.

       H 7 in.   **J** 3 in.

15. 1 cm ... 1 cm ... 1 cm ... |←—4 cm—→|

       A 10 cm   **B** 11 cm

       C 12 cm   **D** 13 cm

Find the area of each figure.

16. |←—5 m—→| 5 m

       F 25 m^2 **G** 25 m^2

       H 15 m^2 **J** 10 m^2

17. |←—— 6 in. ——→| 4 in.

       A 10 in.^{2} **B** 20 in.^{2}

       C 24 in.^{2} **D** 36 in.^{2}

18. 1 cm ... 1 cm ... 1 cm ... |←—4 cm—→|

       F 8 cm^2 **G** 5 cm^2

       H 4 cm^2 **J** 2 cm^2

---

19. What is the volume of a rectangular prism that is 3 ft long, 2 ft high, and 4 ft wide?

   A 6 ft^3 **B** 9 ft^3 **C** 10 ft^3 **D** 24 ft^3

---

20. What two different shapes could be used to form a figure congruent to the one below?

      F square and rectangle   **G** square and triangle

      H square and trapezoid   **J** pentagon and rectangle

Name _____ Date _____

Do you remember?

Use the graph below for Questions 1–4.

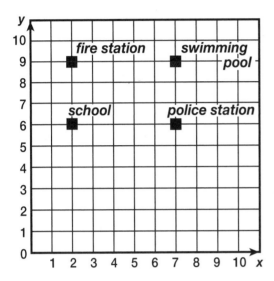

1. You are at the school. Should you go up, down, right, or left to get to the fire station?

   _____

2. You are at the police station. Should you go up, down, right, or left to get to the school?

   _____

3. You are at the fire station. Should you go up, down, right, or left to get to the swimming pool?

   _____

4. You are at the swimming pool. Should you go up, down, right, or left to get to the police station?

   _____

Name _____ Date _____

Use the number line for Questions 5 and 6.

```
        A   B   C   D   E   F   G   H   I
  ◄──┼───┼───┼───┼───┼───┼───┼───┼───┼───┼──►
     0   1   2   3   4   5   6   7   8   9   10
```

5. Write the integer for the letter *C*. _____

6. Write the letter at 6. _____

Use the rule to complete each table.

7.

n	n + 2
1	3
2	4
3	
4	

8.

n	3n
1	3
2	6
3	
4	

Try These!

Write the letter of the point for each ordered pair.

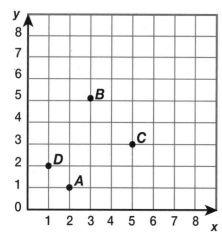

9. (3, 5) _____

10. (2, 1) _____

Plot each point and label it with the correct letter.

11. *F* (3, 1)

12. *K* (7, 5)

Name _____ Date _____

13. Write the pairs of data in the table as ordered pairs. Use the
Number of Packages as the first coordinate.
Graph and connect the ordered pairs to graph the line.

Packages of Pencils

Number of Packages	Number of Pencils
1	2
2	4
3	6
4	8

_____   _____   _____   _____

Packages of Pencils

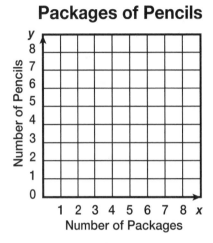

Write the integer for each letter on the number line.

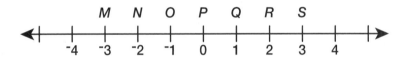

14. *N* _____

15. *R* _____

Find the length of the line segment that connects each pair of points.

16. (2, 3) and (2, 7) _____

17. (3, 8) and (5, 8) _____

Name _____ Date _____

Write the correct answer.

Use the graph for Questions 1–5.

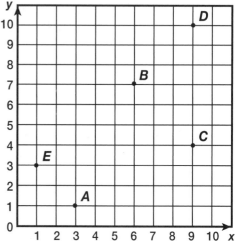

1. Write the letter of the point named by the ordered pair (6, 7). _____

2. Write the letter of the point named by the ordered pair (9, 4). _____

3. What are the coordinates of point *A* ? _____

4. What are the coordinates of point *D* ? _____

5. What are the coordinates of point *E* ? _____

Write the integer for the given letter on the number line.

6. *P* _____

7. *T* _____

8. *V* _____

Let *n* = 3. **Write the correct coordinates for each ordered pair.**

9. (*n*, *n* – 2) _____

10. (*n*, 3*n*) _____

Use the graph for Questions 11–15.

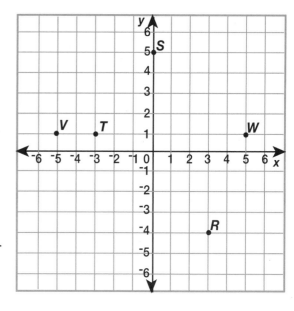

11. Write the letter of the point named by the ordered pair (0, 5). _____

12. Write the point named by the ordered pair (–5, 1). _____

13. What are the coordinates of point *R*? _____

14. What are the coordinates of point *T*? _____

15. What are the coordinates of point *W*? _____

Name _____ Date _____

Find the length of the line segment that connects each pair of points.

16. (4, 2) and (4, 10) _____

17. (−1, 1) and (−1, 7) _____

18. (5, 8) and (8, 8) _____

19. Write an ordered pair that describes a point on the line graphed at right.

_____

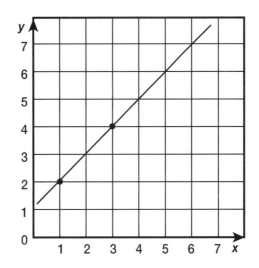

20. How many baseballs would 4 boxes hold?

_____

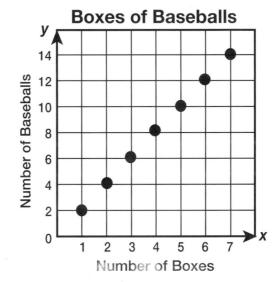

Boxes of Baseballs

Name _____ Date _____

Fill in the ◯ for the correct answer.

Use the graph for Questions 1–5.

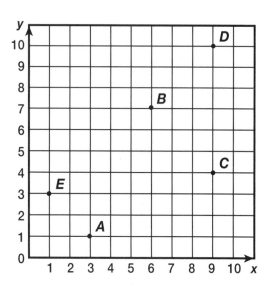

1. Choose the letter of the point named by the ordered pair (6, 7).

   (A) B   (B) C   (C) D   (D) E

2. Choose the letter of the point named by the ordered pair (9, 4).

   (F) A   (G) B   (H) C   (J) D

3. What are the coordinates of point A?

   (A) (3, 1)   (B) (1, 3)   (C) (0, 3)   (D) (3, 0)

4. What are the coordinates of point D?

   (F) (9, 8)   (G) (8, 9)   (H) (10, 9)   (J) (9, 10)

5. What are the coordinates of point E?

   (A) (3, 1)   (B) (1, 3)   (C) (0, 3)   (D) (3, 0)

Write the integer for the given letter on the number line.

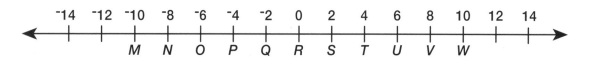

6. P   (F) ⁻8   7. T   (A) ⁻2   8. V   (F) 4

       (G) ⁻6   (B) 0   (G) 6

       (H) ⁻4   (C) 2   (H) 8

       (J) ⁻2   (D) 4   (J) 10

Name _____   Date _____

Let _n_ = 3. Choose the correct coordinates for each ordered pair.

9. (_n_, _n_ − 2)

  A (3, −6)   **B** (3, 1)   **C** (3, 5)   **D** (3, 6)

10. (_n_, 3_n_)

  F (3, 9)   **G** (3, 6)   **H** (3, 0)   **J** (3, −6)

Use the graph below for Questions 11–15.

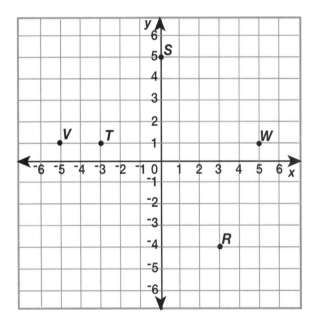

11. Choose the letter of the point named by the ordered pair (0, 10).

  A _R_   **B** _S_

  C _T_   **D** _V_

12. Choose the letter of the point named by the ordered pair (−5, 1).

  F _S_   **G** _T_

  H _V_   **J** _W_

13. What are the coordinates of point _R_?

  A (3, 4)   **B** (3, −4)   **C** (−4, 3)   **D** (–4, 3)

14. What are the coordinates of point _T_?

  F (−3, 1)   **G** (−1, 3)   **H** (1, −3)   **J** (3, −1)

15. What are the coordinates of point _W_?

  A (5, 1)   **B** (1, 5)   **C** (1, −5)   **D** (−5, 1)

Name _____ Date _____

Find the length of the line segment that connects each pair of points.

16. (4, 2) and (4, 10)

(F) 8   (G) 12   (H) 16   (J) 20

17. (−1, 1) and (−1, 7)

(A) 2   (B) 6   (C) 8   (D) 9

18. (5, 8) and (8, 8)

(F) 0   (G) 3   (H) 13   (J) 16

19. Which ordered pair describes a point on the line graphed on the right?

(A) (1, 2)   (B) (1, 3)

(C) (2, 1)   (D) (3, 1)

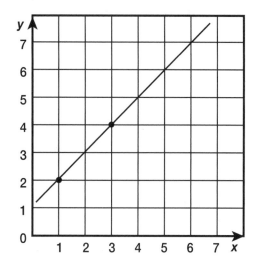

Use the graph to solve the problem.

20. How many baseballs would 4 boxes hold?

(F) 4   (G) 6

(H) 8   (J) 10

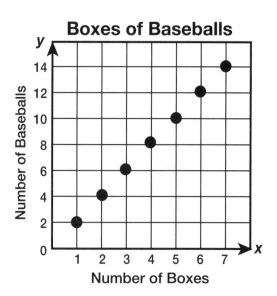

Boxes of Baseballs

Name _____ Date _____

Write the correct answer.

Do you remember?

Add, subtract, multiply, or divide.

1. $9 + 4 =$ _____ **2.** $4 + 8 =$ _____

3. $4 + 7 =$ _____ **4.** $9 + 6 =$ _____

5. $15 - 8 =$ _____ **6.** $12 - 7 =$ _____

7. $13 - 5 =$ _____ **8.** $16 - 7 =$ _____

9. $6 \times 7 =$ _____ **10.** $7 \times 4 =$ _____

11. $8 \times 8 =$ _____ **12.** $3 \times 8 =$ _____

13. $32 \div 4 =$ _____ **14.** $63 \div 7 =$ _____

15. $49 \div 7 =$ _____ **16.** $24 \div 6 =$ _____

17. $6\overline{)64}$ **18.** $9\overline{)297}$

Name _____   Date _____

Try These!

Use basic facts to help you divide.

19. $70\overline{)4,900}$

20. $40\overline{)24,000}$

Divide.

21. $42\overline{)252}$

22. $39\overline{)314}$

---

23. $19\overline{)503}$

24. $63\overline{)4,671}$

---

25. $915 \div 36 =$ _____

26. $869 \div 17 =$ _____

---

27. $576 \div 28 =$ _____

28. $2,192 \div 54 =$ _____

Estimate the quotient.

29. $28\overline{)267}$

30. $67\overline{)559}$

Name _____ Date _____

Fill in the ◯ for the correct answer.

Use basic facts to help you divide.

1. 70)‾56,000   (A) 8,000   (B) 800   (C) 80   (D) 8

2. 6)‾2,400   (F) 4,000   (G) 400   (H) 40   (J) 4

Divide.

3. 18)‾72   (A) 2   (B) 3   (C) 4   (D) 6

4. 78)‾702   (F) 6   (G) 7   (H) 8   (J) 9

5. 39)‾195   (A) 5   (B) 4   (C) 3   (D) 2

6. 27)‾93   (F) 30 R 12   (G) 4 R 5   (H) 3 R 12   (J) 3 R 3

7. 59)‾248   (A) 4 R 8   (B) 4 R 12   (C) 5 R 53   (D) 40 R 12

8. 52)‾425   (F) 8 R 9   (G) 8 R 25   (H) 80 R 9   (J) 80 R 25

Which symbol makes each statement true?

9. 728 ÷ 28 ⬤ 728 ÷ 82   (A) >   (B) <   (C) =   (D) +

10. 360 ÷ 40 ⬤ 540 ÷ 60   (F) >   (G) <   (H) =   (J) +

Divide.

11. 23)‾742   (A) 320 R 6   (B) 36 R 14   (C) 32 R 14   (D) 32 R 6

12. 46)‾992   (F) 19 R 18   (G) 20 R 2   (H) 21 R 26   (J) 22 R 20

13. 38)‾2,136   (A) 49 R 34   (B) 56 R 8   (C) 56 R 12   (D) 506 R 8

14. 92)‾6,729   (F) 73 R 13   (G) 73 R 53   (H) 704 R 61   (J) 730 R 13

15. 39)‾774   (A) 13 R 3   (B) 19 R 33   (C) 20 R 14   (D) 22 R 26

16. 43)‾819   (F) 23 R 30   (G) 21 R 16   (H) 19 R 42   (J) 19 R 2

Name _____ Date _____

Divide.

17. $2,014 \div 68 =$ ▢   (A) 25 R 14   (B) 29 R 42   (C) 30 R 34   (D) 32 R 48

18. $8,113 \div 92 =$ ▢   (F) 88 R 17   (G) 88 R 27   (H) 89 R 25   (J) 90 R 73

19. $703 \div 64 =$ ▢   (A) 12 R 45   (B) 12 R 25   (C) 11 R 1   (D) 10 R 63

20. $792 \div 38 =$ ▢   (F) 2 R 32   (G) 20 R 13   (H) 20 R 32   (J) 21 R 6

21. $5,209 \div 74 =$ ▢   (A) 72 R 41   (B) 71 R 55   (C) 70 R 29   (D) 7 R 29

22. $4,703 \div 52 =$ ▢   (F) 90 R 23   (G) 91 R 31   (H) 94 R 15   (J) 95 R 33

Solve.

23. There are 118 fourth grade students and 143 fifth grade students who eat lunch at the same time. If 12 students can sit at one lunch table, how many tables are needed to seat all of the students?

(A) 37 tables   (B) 25 tables   (C) 22 tables   (D) 20 tables

24. A bakery bakes 875 loaves of bread each day. Each loaf is sliced and is cut 19 times. How many slices of bread do they have in all ?

(F) 17,500 slices   (G) 16,625 slices   (H) 894 slices   (J) 856 slices

25. The cafeteria serves 1,840 cartons of milk each week. If the same number of cartons are served each day, how many cartons are served in one day?

(A) 206 cartons   (B) 260 cartons   (C) 316 cartons   (D) 368 cartons

Name _____ Date _____

Choose the correct answer.

1. What is the word form of 62,008,429?

   (A) sixty-two million, 8 thousand, four hundred twenty nine

   (B) sixty-two billion, 8 million, four hundred twenty nine

   (C) six billion, two million, eight thousand, four hundred twenty nine

   (D) six hundred two million, eight thousand, four hundred twenty nine

Which symbol makes each statement true?

2. 588,700 ⬤ 587,800   (F) >   (G) <   (H) =   (J) +

3. 3,040,600 ⬤ 3,100,600   (A) >   (B) <   (C) =   (D) +

---

4. Which numbers are ordered from least to greatest?

   (F) 74,085   72,085   72,580   (G) 72,580   72,085   74,085

   (H) 72,085   74,085   72,580   (J) 72,085   72,580   74,085

---

5. Round 254,718 to the nearest ten thousand.

   (A) 240,000   (B) 250,000   (C) 254,000   (D) 255,000

---

6. Thomasine bought fruit for $5.12. She paid with a $10 bill. What change should she have received?

   (F) 3 pennies, 1 dime, 1 quarter, 1 half-dollar, 5 one dollar bills

   (G) 3 pennies, 1 dime, 2 quarters, 4 one dollar bills

   (H) 3 pennies, 1 dime, 1 quarter, 1 half-dollar, 4 one dollar bills

   (J) 3 pennies, 3 dimes, 1 half-dollar, 4 one dollar bills

Name _____ Date _____

7. Anna, Bryce, Clara, Drake, and Emily are standing in line for theater tickets. Anna is standing next to Drake. Emily is in front of Anna. Clara is standing between Drake and Bryce. Who is last in line?

   (A) Anna   (B) Bryce   (C) Clara   (D) Emily

8. Complete the number sentence. Which property of addition did you use?

   $15 + (5 + 38) = ($ ▢ $+ 5) + 38$

   (F) 5; associative   (G) 15; associative   (H) 5; commutative   (J) 15; commutative

9. 4,075   (A) 4,993   (B) 5,003   (C) 5,093   (D) 5,993
    + 928

10. 26,714   (F) 59,239   (G) 60,239   (H) 69,239   (J) 160,239
    + 33,525

11. 18,004   (A) 10,898   (B) 10,998   (C) 10,902   (D) 11,102
    − 7,106

12. Simplify the expression.

    $(16 − 4) + (12 − 1)$ (F) 33   (G) 25   (H) 23   (J) 1

13. Find the value of y when $x = 2$ for the following equation.

    $y = 10 − x$ (A) 5   (B) 8   (C) 12   (D) 20

14. Solve the equation.

    $m + 5 = 15$ (F) 3   (G) 10   (H) 20   (J) 75

15. Marcy bought a sandwich for $4.19 and a glass of milk for $0.89. How much change should she get back from a $20 bill?

    (A) $14.92   (B) $14.98   (C) $15.08   (D) $15.92

Name _____ Date _____

Find each product.

16. $4 \times 8 =$ ▢   (F) 12   (G) 24   (H) 28   (J) 32

17. $8 \times 5 =$ ▢   (A) 13   (B) 40   (C) 45   (D) 50

18. $7 \times 6 =$ ▢   (F) 13   (G) 36   (H) 42   (J) 56

Find each quotient and remainder.

19. $45 \div 8 =$ ▢   (A) 5 R5   (B) 5 R3   (C) 4 R5   (D) 4 R3

20. $38 \div 9 =$ ▢   (F) 3 R2   (G) 3 R7   (H) 4 R2   (J) 4 R7

21. $19 \div 4 =$ ▢   (A) 3 R7   (B) 4 R1   (C) 4 R3   (D) 5 R1

22. Solve the equation. Name the property that you used.

$(9 \times 8) \times 5 = a \times (8 \times 5)$

(F) 9; Associative Property   (G) 9; Commutative Property

(H) 5; Associative Property   (J) 5; Commutative Property

23. Evaluate the expression when $k = 6$.

$5k - 3$ (A) 6   (B) 12   (C) 24   (D) 27

24. Solve.

$n \div 8 = 7$ (F) 54   (G) 56   (H) 57   (J) not possible

25. William saved $8 this week. If he continues to save the same amount for 6 weeks, how much will he have altogether?

(A) $2   (B) $14   (C) $24   (D) $48

Name _____   Date _____

Choose the correct answer for each.

Multiply.

1. 5,000
      × 300

- (A) 15,000
- (B) 150,000
- (C) 1,500,000
- (D) 15,000,000

2. 74
      × 8

- (F) 562
- (G) 592
- (H) 862
- (J) 5,632

3. 837
      × 4

- (A) 3,348
- (B) 3,528
- (C) 3,548
- (D) 321,228

4. $408
      × 7

- (F) $28,056
- (G) $28,506
- (H) $20,856
- (J) $2,856

5. 8,000
      × 7

- (A) 5,600
- (B) 56,000
- (C) 560,000
- (D) 5,600,000

6. 56
      × 21

- (F) 168
- (G) 1,168
- (H) 1,176
- (J) 11,256

7. 659
      × 35

- (A) 2,365
- (B) 5,272
- (C) 23,065
- (D) 484,072

8. Which operation would you use to solve the following problem?
Six friends each want 3 slices of pizza. How many pieces should they order?

- (F) addition
- (G) subtraction
- (H) multiplication
- (J) division

Divide.

9. 6)72

- (A) 1 R12
- (B) 10 R12
- (C) 11 R12
- (D) 12

10. 4)2,400

- (F) 6
- (G) 60
- (H) 600
- (J) 6,000

Name _____ Date _____

Divide.

11. 8)956

(A) 17 (B) 117 (C) 119 R4 (D) 122

12. 7)3,009

(F) 44 R1 (g) 429 R6 (h) 4,029 R6 (J) 4,287

13. Which number is divisible by 2, 5, and 10?

(A) 30 (B) 35 (C) 55 (D) all of these

14. Which list contains only prime numbers?

(F) 2, 4, 6, 8, 10 (G) 2, 3, 5, 7, 9 (H) 3, 5, 7, 9, 11 (J) 2, 3, 5, 7, 11

15. Find the average of the following numbers.

40, 44, 45, 50, 51

(A) 11 (B) 45 (C) 46 (D) 48

16. Dora is packaging pens. She has 38 pens to package. If 8 pens fit in each package, how many will she have left over?

(F) 0 (G) 4 (H) 6 (J) 8

17. The fourth grade class is planning a picnic at the end of the year. They will use vans to transport everyone to the picnic area. There are 30 students in the class. Each van holds 5 students. How many vans will they need?

(A) 6 (B) 25 (C) 35 (D) 150

Choose the missing number.

18. 4 miles = ⬜ feet

(F) 21,120 (G) 8,000 (H) 4,000 (J) 1,320

Name _____ Date _____

Choose the missing number.

19. 12 cm = ▮ mm

(A) 120   (B) 1,200   (C) 12,000   (D) 12,000,000

---

20. 8 pounds = ▮ ounces

(F) 2   (G) 16   (H) 80   (J) 128

---

21. 12 feet = ▮ yards

(A) 2   (B) 3   (C) 4   (D) 6

---

22. 5,000 milliliters = ▮ liters

(F) 5   (G) 500   (H) 5,000   (J) 5,000,000

---

23. 4 gallons = ▮ quarts

(A) 2   (B) 8   (C) 16   (D) 24

---

24. What is the temperature?

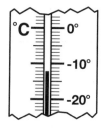

(F) 12° C   (G) 8° C   (H) ⁻8° C   (J) ⁻12° C

25. The temperature in Seattle was 56° F when Jenna called Mitchell in New York. Mitchell told her that the temperature was 19° cooler in New York than in Seattle. What was the temperature in New York?

(A) 37° F   (B) 43° F   (C) 47° F   (D) 75° F

Name _____ Date _____

Choose the correct answer for each.

1. Find $\frac{3}{4}$ of 12.

(A) 8 (B) 9 (C) 36 (D) 48

2. Which mixed number is the same as $\frac{23}{4}$?

(F) $5\frac{4}{3}$ (G) $5\frac{3}{4}$ (H) $5\frac{1}{4}$ (J) $2\frac{3}{4}$

3. Which fraction is the same as $\frac{12}{18}$ in simplest form?

(A) $\frac{1}{7}$ (B) $\frac{1}{3}$ (C) $\frac{2}{3}$ (D) $\frac{4}{6}$

Which symbol makes each statement true?

4. $\frac{7}{16}$ ⬤ $\frac{9}{16}$ (F) >   (G) <   (H) =   (J) +

5. $\frac{4}{12}$ ⬤ $\frac{7}{21}$ (A) >   (B) <   (C) =   (D) +

Add or subtract. Write the sum or difference in simplest form.

6. $\frac{3}{8}$
$+\frac{1}{8}$

(F) $\frac{1}{2}$ (G) $\frac{1}{4}$
(H) $\frac{1}{3}$ (J) $\frac{4}{8}$

7. $4\frac{5}{6}$
$-3\frac{1}{6}$

(A) $2\frac{2}{3}$ (B) $1\frac{2}{3}$
(C) $1\frac{4}{6}$ (D) $\frac{2}{3}$

8. Andrew, Beth, Clark, and Dana are sitting at a round table. Andrew is not sitting next to Beth. Who is sitting next to Clark?

(F) Andrew and Dana

(G) Dana and Beth

(H) Andrew and Beth

(J) Only Dana

Name _____ Date _____

9. Which fraction or mixed number is the same as 3.25?

(A) $3\frac{2}{5}$ (B) $3\frac{25}{100}$ (C) $3\frac{1}{25}$ (D) $\frac{3}{25}$

10. Which decimal number is the same as $5\frac{42}{100}$?

(F) 0.0542 (G) 0.542 (H) 5.42 (J) 54.2

Which symbol makes each statement true?

11. 8.12 ⬤ 8.3 (A) > (B) < (C) = (D) +

12. 2.500 ⬤ 2.5 (F) > (G) < (H) = (J) +

13.
$$\begin{array}{r} 15.28 \\ + 12.07 \\ \hline \end{array}$$
(A) 27.35 (B) 27.45 (C) 28.25 (D) 37.25

14.
$$\begin{array}{r} 456.19 \\ - 318.47 \\ \hline \end{array}$$
(F) 137.72 (G) 138.72 (H) 142.32 (J) 148.72

15.
$$\begin{array}{r} 21.05 \\ - 13.27 \\ \hline \end{array}$$
(A) 12.88 (B) 12.82 (C) 8.78 (D) 7.78

16. Round 56.3495 to the nearest tenth.

(F) 56.2 (G) 56.3 (H) 56.34 (J) 56.35

17. Dennis bought a 3.35-pound package of ground turkey. His recipe calls for 5 pounds of ground turkey. How much more does he need?

(A) 8.35 pounds (B) 2.35 pounds (C) 1.35 pounds (D) 1.65 pounds

Name _____ Date _____

**Order the data from least to greatest. Find the range, mode, median, and mean.
Then identify any outliers.**

18. 9, 6, 6, 4, 2, 3

(F) range = 4
mode = 6
median = 5
mean = 6
no outliers

(G) range = 7
mode = 6
median = 5
mean = 6
outlier = 9

(H) range = 7
mode = 6
median = 5
mean = 7
outlier = 9

(J) range = 7
mode = 6
median = 5
mean = 5
no outliers

19. 20, 5, 25, 35, 25

(A) range = 5
mode = 25
median = 25
mean = 25
outlier = 20

(B) range = 5
mode = 25
median = 25
mean = 22
outlier = 5

(C) range = 30
mode = 25
median = 25
mean = 22
outlier = 5

(D) range = 30
mode = 25
median = 25
mean = 22
outlier = 20

Use the graph for Questions 20 and 21.

20. If 32° F is freezing, which days were below freezing?

(F) only Tuesday

(G) Wednesday, Thursday, Friday

(H) Wednesday and Friday

(J) only Thursday

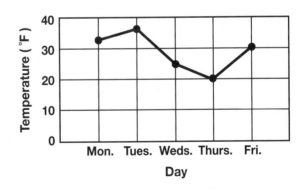

21. Describe the temperature change from Tuesday to Wednesday.

(A) The temperature dropped about 10 degrees.

(B) The temperature increased about 10 degrees.

(C) The temperature dropped about 5 degrees.

(D) The temperature increased about 5 degrees.

Name _____ Date _____

A bag contains 3 blue marbles, 1 red marble, and 6 yellow marbles. Choose certain, likely, unlikely, or impossible for Questions 22 and 23.

22. What is the probability of choosing a white marble from the bag?

(F) certain   (G) likely   (H) unlikely   (J) impossible

23. What is the probability of choosing a yellow marble from the bag?

(A) certain   (B) likely   (C) unlikely   (D) impossible

You write each of the letters C, H, O, O, S, E, O, N, and E on a card and place the cards in a bag.

24. If you pick one card without looking, which cards will you probably pick the most often?

(F) C and E   (G) C and O   (H) O and E   (J) C, O, and E

25. If you pick a card and put it back 27 times, how many times would you probably pick the letter H?

(A) 3 times   (B) 9 times   (C) 12 times   (D) 27 times

Name _____   Date _____

Choose the correct name for the figure.

1.

    (**A**) equilateral triangle   (**B**) acute scalene triangle

    (**C**) right scalene triangle   (**D**) right isosceles triangle

---

2.

    (**F**) parallelogram   (**G**) rectangle

    (**H**) square   (**J**) trapezoid

---

3. How many lines of symmetry does this figure have?

    (**A**) 1   (**B**) 2

    (**C**) 3   (**D**) 4

---

4. Find the perimeter of this figure.

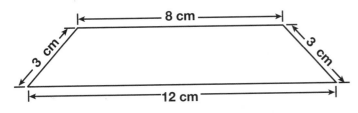

    (**F**) 20   (**G**) 26

    (**H**) 24   (**J**) 36

---

5. Find the perimeter of the square.

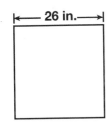

    (**A**) 26 in.   (**B**) 52 in.

    (**C**) 104 in.   (**D**) 208 in.

---

6. Find the area of the rectangle.

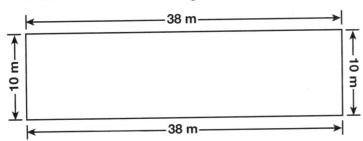

    (**F**) 48 m^2 (**G**) 192 m^2

    (**H**) 96 m^2 (**J**) 380 m^2

Name _____ Date _____

Use this figure for Questions 7 and 8.

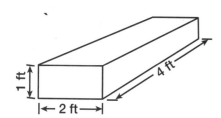

7. Find the volume of the figure.

   (A) 4 ft³   (B) 7 ft³

   (C) 8 ft³   (D) 16 ft³

8. Find the surface area of the figure.

   (F) 7 ft²   (G) 8 ft²   (H) 14 ft²   (J) 28 ft²

9. A box is 2 m high, 1.5 m wide, and 1 m long. It is half full of sand. How many cubic meters of sand is it holding?

   (A) 1.5 m³   (B) 2 m³   (C) 3 m³   (D) 4 m³

Use the graph for Questions 10 – 14.

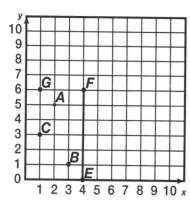

10. Which letter is at (5, 2)?

    (F) A   (G) B

    (H) C   (J) D

11. What are the coordinates of point B?

    (A) (1, 1)   (B) (1, 3)

    (C) (3, 1)   (D) (3, 3)

12. What are the coordinates of point G?

    (F) (1, 1)   (G) (1, 6)   (H) (6, 1)   (J) (6, 6)

13. What is the length of the segment that connects points E and F?

    (A) 2 units   (B) 4 units   (C) 6 units   (D) 8 units

14. Which ordered pair represents a point on the segment whose endpoints are E and F?

    (F) (4, 5)   (G) (5, 4)   (H) (3, 0)   (J) (0, 3)

Name _____ Date _____

Use the number line for Questions 15 and 16. Write the integer for the given letter on the number line.

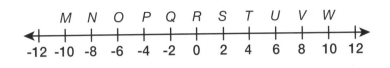

15. *P*

(A) 4　　　　(B) − 2　　　　(C) − 4　　　　(D) − 6

16. *M*

(F) − 10　　　(G) − 8　　　(H) 8　　　(J) 10

17. Peggy, Quentin, and Richard each sent an e-mail to each of the other two. How many letters did they send among each other altogether?

(A) 2　　　　(B) 3　　　　(C) 4　　　　(D) 6

Divide.

18. 30)1200

(F) 4　　　(G) 40

(H) 400　　(J) 4,000

19. 50)750

(A) 15　　(B) 150

(C) 1,500　(D) 15,000

20. 22)1,955

(F) 87 R3　(G) 87 R19

(H) 88 R3　(J) 88 R19

21. 72)1,324

(A) 17 R44　(B) 18 R28

(C) 18 R44　(D) 19 R28

22. 68)3,111

(F) 44 R17　(G) 44 R51

(H) 45 R17　(J) 45 R51

23. 51)2,555

(A) 49 R56　(B) 50 R5

(C) 50 R46　(D) 51 R46

24. Ramona bought a milkshake for $1.80, a hamburger for $4.15, and a salad for $2.50. How much change should she receive from a $20 bill?

(F) $11.55　　(G) $15.85　　(H) $17.50　　(J) $18.20

25. Mariette has a 20-foot piece of ribbon. How many cuts does she need to make to cut 10 pieces of ribbon from it?

(A) 2　　　　(B) 9　　　　(C) 10　　　　(D) 11

Name _____ Date _____

Write the correct answer.

1. Compare 426,345 and 426,305. Use $<$, $>$, or $=$.

   _____

2. Round 872,568 to the nearest hundred thousand.

   _____

3. Add.

   $$\begin{array}{r} 6,463 \\ +\ \ 349 \\ \hline \end{array}$$

4. Subtract.

   $$\begin{array}{r} 15,156 \\ -\ 6,248 \\ \hline \end{array}$$

5. Subtract.

   $23,000 - 5,020 =$

   _____

6. Simplify.

   $(16 + 3) + (18 - 2) =$

   _____

7. Solve the equation. Name the property that you used.

   $7 \times 8 = m \times 7$

   _____

8. Evaluate the expression

   $24 \div n$ when $n = 6$.

   _____

Multiply.

9. $\begin{array}{r} 308 \\ \times\ \ \ 7 \\ \hline \end{array}$

10. $\begin{array}{r} 45 \\ \times\ 26 \\ \hline \end{array}$

Divide.

11. $6\overline{)2,922}$

12. Which number is prime?

   6   9   13   18

   _____

13. Find the perimeter of the figure.

   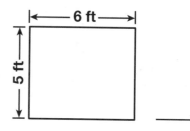

   _____

Name _____   Date _____

14. Fill in the missing number.

24 inches = _____ feet

15. Write the mixed number for the improper fraction.

$\frac{9}{7}$ _____

16. Add. Write the sum in simplest form.

$\frac{3}{8} + \frac{1}{8} =$ _____

17. Subtract. Write the difference in simplest form.

$\frac{11}{12} - \frac{9}{12} =$ _____

18. Compare 3.09 and 3.9. Use < , > , or = . _____

19. Add.

6.3
+5.9

20. Subtract.

15.4
− 9.6

21. Order the data from least to greatest. Find the range, mode, median, and mean.

6   9   4   6   5

_____

_____

22. Name the figure.

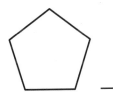

_____

23. Find the area of the figure.

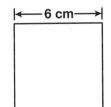

|←——6 cm——→|

_____

24. Write the integer for *B* on the number line.

_____

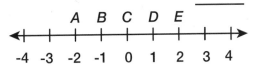

25. Divide.

1,106 ÷ 46 = _____

Name _____ **Date** _____

Chapter 1 Test

Form A   Form B

Total Test Score _____ _____

Percent Correct Score _____ _____

Objectives	Student Pages	Form A Items	Number Correct	Form B Items	Number Correct
1A Read, write and identify place value of a digit in whole numbers through hundred millions	4–5, 16–19	1–7		1–7	
1B Compare, order, and round numbers	6–8, 10–11, 20–22, 24–25	8–18		8–18	
1C Find and compare values of collections of bills and coins; make change	30–32, 34–35	19–22		19–22	
1D Analyze and solve problems using skills and strategies	12–13, 26–27, 36–37	23–25		23–25	

Total Test Score _____ _____

Name _____   **Date** _____

Chapter 2 Test

	Form A	Form B

Total Test Score _____   _____

Percent Correct Score _____   _____

	Objectives	Student Pages	Form A Items	Number Correct	Form B Items	Number Correct
2A	Use properties of addition	54–55	1–2		1–2	
2B	Add and subtract three-, four-, and five-digit whole numbers; estimate sums and differences	56–58, 60–62, 64–65, 68–69	3–14		3–14	
2C	Write expressions and equations; use addition and subtraction to evaluate expressions, and solve equations	74–80, 82–87	15–22		15–22	
2D	Analyze and solve problems using skills and strategies	66–67, 70–71, 88–89	23–25		23–25	

Total Test Score _____   _____

Name _____   Date _____

Chapter 3 Test

Form A   **Form B**

Total Test Score _____   _____

Percent Correct Score _____   _____

	Objectives	Student Pages	Form A Items	Number Correct	Form B Items	Number Correct
3A	Multiply and divide by 2, 3, 4, 5, 6, 7, 8, 9, or 10	106–108, 112–114, 118–121, 124–127	1–13		1–13	
3B	Use properties and rules of multiplication and division	110–111, 122–123	14–17		14–17	
3C	Write expressions and equations, evaluate expressions and functions, and solve equations	132–134, 136–138, 142–146	18–23		18–23	
3D	Analyze and solve problems using skills and strategies	128–129, 140–141, 148–149	24–25		24–25	

Total Test Score _____   _____

Name _____   Date _____

Chapter 4 Test

Form A   Form B

Total Test Score _____   _____

Percent Correct Score _____   _____

Objectives		Student Pages	Form A Items	Number Correct	Form B Items	Number Correct
4A	Multiply one-, two-, three-, and four-digit numbers by 1-digit numbers and estimate products	166–172, 174–175, 180–184, 186–187	1–17		1–17	
4B	Multiply 2- and 3-digit numbers by 2-digit numbers	192–196, 198–199	18–22		18–22	
4C	Analyze and solve problems using skills and strategies	176–177, 188–189, 200–201	23–25		23–25	

Total Test Score _____   _____

Name _____ Date _____

Chapter 5 Test

	Form A	Form B
Total Test Score	_____	_____
Percent Correct Score	_____	_____

	Objectives	Student Pages	Form A Items	Number Correct	Form B Items	Number Correct
5A	Divide two- and three-digit dividends with two-digit, three-digit, and four-digit quotients and estimate quotients	218–224, 230–240, 254–258	1–17		1–17	
5B	Apply divisibility rules for division by 2, 5, and 10; identify prime and composite numbers	246–249	18–21		18–21	
5C	Find the average of a set of numbers	250–253	22–23		22–23	
5D	Analyze and solve problems using skills and strategies	226–227, 242–243, 260–263	24–25		24–25	

Total Test Score _____   _____

Name _____   Date _____

Chapter 6 Test

Form A   Form B

Total Test Score _____   _____

Percent Correct Score _____   _____

	Objectives	Student Pages	Form A Items	Number Correct	Form B Items	Number Correct
6A	Measure lengths and find perimeters using customary and metric units	278–281, 290–293	1–6, 11–13,15		1–6, 11–13,15	
6B	Convert among units of capacity and weight (mass) and choose the most appropriate unit of capacity and mass	282–285, 294–296	7–10, 14,16		7–10 14,16	
6C	Measure temperature above and below zero using degrees Fahrenheit and degrees Celsius	302–305	17–18		17–18	
6D	Analyze and solve problems using skills and strategies	286–287, 298–299, 306–307	19–20		19–20	

Total Test Score _____   _____

Name _____ Date _____

Chapter 7 Test

Form A   Form B

Total Test Score _____   _____

Percent Correct Score _____   _____

	Objectives	Student Pages	Form A Items	Number Correct	Form B Items	Number Correct
7A	Represent a fraction of a region, of a set, and of a number; write mixed numbers	324–327, 342–345	1–8		1–8	
7B	Find equivalent fractions	328–332	9–13		9–13	
7C	Compare and order fractions	338–340	14–15		14–15	
7D	Add and subtract fractions with like denominators	350–353	16–23		16–23	
7E	Analyze and solve problems using skills and strategies	334–335, 346–347, 354–355	24–25		24–25	

Total Test Score _____   _____

Name _____ **Date** _____

Chapter 8 Test

Form A   Form B

Total Test Score _____   _____

Percent Correct Score _____   _____

	Objectives	Student Pages	Form A Items	Number Correct	Form B Items	Number Correct
8A	Write fractions and mixed numbers as decimals and vice-versa	372–376, 378–379	1–5		1–5	
8B	Compare and order fractions, mixed numbers, and decimals	380–383	6–11		6–11	
8C	Add and subtract decimals	388–389	12–16		12–16	
8D	Round decimals and estimate sums and differences of decimals	392–396	17–22		17–22	
8E	Analyze and solve problems using skills and strategies	384–385, 390–391, 398–399	23–25		23–25	

Total Test Score _____   _____

Name _____ Date _____

Chapter 9 Test

Form A   Form B

Total Test Score _____   _____

Percent Correct Score _____   _____

	Objectives	Student Pages	Form A Items	Number Correct	Form B Items	Number Correct
9A	Find mean, median, and mode of numerical data	418–420	1–2		1–2	
9B	Make, read, and interpret a bar graph	416–417, 422–424	3–6		3–6	
9C	Read a line graph	428–429	7–10		7–10	
9D	Describe the probability of an event and determine the number of possible outcomes in an experiment	434–441	11–18		11–18	
9E	Analyze and solve problems using skills and strategies	426–427, 430–432, 442–443	19–20		19–20	

Total Test Score _____   _____

Name _____   **Date** _____

Chapter 10 Test

			Form A		Form B	
	Objectives	**Student Pages**	**Form A Items**	**Number Correct**	**Form B Items**	**Number Correct**
10A	Identify plane and solid geometric figures	460–462, 464–471, 498–500	1–9		1–9	
10B	Identify congruent figures and figures with line and rotational symmetry	474–476, 478–481	10–11		10–11	
10C	Find perimeter and area	486–490 492–493	12–18		12–18	
10D	Find the surface area and volume of a rectangular prism	502–505	19		19	
10E	Analyze and solve problems using skills and strategies	482–483, 494–496, 506–507	20		20	

Total Test Score _____   _____

Total Test Score _____   _____

Percent Correct Score _____   _____

Form A   Form B

Name _____ **Date** _____

Chapter 11 Test

Form A   Form B

Total Test Score _____   _____

Percent Correct Score _____   _____

	Objectives	Student Pages	Form A Items	Number Correct	Form B Items	Number Correct
11A	Locate, identify, and graph points on a coordinate plane and find the distance between two points	524–527, 538–544, 548–549	1–18		1–18	
11B	Graph lines	528–530	19		19	
11C	Analyze and solve problems using skills and strategies	532–533, 536–537, 546–547, 550–551	20		20	

Total Test Score _____   _____

Name _____   **Date** _____

Chapter 12 Test

Form A   Form B

Total Test Score _____   _____

Percent Correct Score _____   _____

	Objectives	Student Pages	Form A Items	Number Correct	Form B Items	Number Correct
12A	Divide by multiples of 10	568–569	1–2		1–2	
12B	Divide and estimate quotients with 2-digit, 3-digit, and 4-digit dividends with 1- and 2-digit quotients	570–572, 574–575, 580–582, 584–585, 588–589	3–22		3–22	
12C	Analyze and solve problems using skills and strategies	576–577, 586–587, 590–591	23–25		23–25	

Total Test Score _____   _____

Name _____ Date _____

Quarterly Test 1

Total Test Score _____

Chapters 1–3

Percent Correct Score _____

Objectives	Student Pages	Items	Number Correct
1A Read, write and identify place value of a digit in whole numbers through hundred millions	4–5, 16–19	1	
1B Compare, order, and round numbers	6–8, 10–11, 20–22, 24–25	2–5	
1C Find and compare values of collections of bills and coins; make change	30–32, 34–35	6–15	
2A Use properties of addition	54–55	8	
2B Add and subtract three-, four-, and five-digit whole numbers; estimate sums and differences	56–58, 60–62, 64–65, 68–69	9–11	
2C Write expressions and equations; use addition and subtraction to evaluate expressions, and solve equations	74–80, 82–87	12–14	
3A Multiply and divide by 2, 3, 4, 5, 6, 7, 8, 9, or 10	106–108, 112–114, 118–121, 124–127	16–21	
3B Use properties and rules of multiplication and division	110–111, 122–123	22	
3C Write expressions and equations, evaluate expressions and functions, and solve equations	132–134, 136–138, 142–146	22–24	
1D, 2D, 3D Analyze and solve problems using skills and strategies	12–13, 26–27, 36–37, 66–67, 70–71, 88–89, 128–129, 140–141, 148–149	7, 25	

Total Test Score _____

Name _____   Date _____

Quarterly Test 2

Total Test Score _____

Chapters 4–6

Percent Correct Score _____

Objectives	Student Pages	Items	Number Correct
4A Multiply one-, two-, three-, and four-digit numbers by 1-digit numbers and estimate products	166–172, 174–175, 180–184, 186–187	1–5	
4B Multiply 2- and 3-digit numbers by 2-digit numbers	192–196, 198–199	6–7	
5A Divide two- and three-digit dividends with two-digit, three-digit, and four-digit quotients and estimate quotients	218–224, 230–240, 254–258	9–12	
5B Apply divisibility rules for division by 2, 5, and 10; identify prime and composite numbers	246–249	13–14	
5C Find the average of a set of numbers	250–253	15	
6A Measure lengths and find perimeters using customary and metric units	278–281, 290–293	18–19, 21	
6B Convert among units of capacity and weight (mass) and choose the most appropriate unit of capacity and mass	282–285, 294–296	20, 22–23	
6C Measure temperature above and below zero using degrees Fahrenheit and degrees Celsius	302–305	24	
4C, 5D, 6D Analyze and solve problems using skills and strategies	176–177, 188–189, 200–201, 226–227, 242–243, 260–263, 286–287, 298–299, 306–307	8, 16–17, 25	

Total Test Score _____

Name _____   **Date** _____

Quarterly Test 3

Chapters 7–9

Total Test Score _____

Percent Correct Score _____

	Objectives	Student Pages	Items	Number Correct
7A	Represent a fraction of a region, of a set, and of a number; write mixed numbers	324–327, 342–345	1–2	
7B	Find equivalent fractions	328–332	3	
7C	Compare and order fractions	338–340	4–5	
7D	Add and subtract fractions with like denominators	350–353	6–7	
8A	Write fractions and mixed numbers as decimals and vice-versa	372–376, 378–379	9–10	
8B	Compare and order fractions, mixed numbers, and decimals	380–383	11–12	
8C	Add and subtract decimals	388–389	13–14	
8D	Round decimals and estimate sums and differences of decimals	392–396	16	
9A	Find mean, median, and mode of numerical data	418–420	18–19	
9B	Make, read, and interpret a bar graph	416–417, 422–424	20	
9C	Read a line graph	428–429	21	
9D	Describe the probability of an event and determine the number of possible outcomes in an experiment	434–441	22–25	
7E, 8E, 9E	Analyze and solve problems using skills and strategies	334–335, 346–347, 354–355, 384–385, 390–391, 398–399, 426–427, 430–431, 442–443	8, 17	

Total Test Score _____

Name _____ Date _____

Quarterly Test 4

Chapters 10–12

Total Test Score _____

Percent Correct Score _____

Objectives	Student Pages	Items	Number Correct
10A Identify plane and solid geometric figures	460–462, 464–471, 498–500	1–2	
10B Identify congruent figures and figures with line and rotational symmetry	474–476, 478–481	3	
10C Find perimeter and area	486–490, 492–493	4–6	
10D Find the surface area and volume of a rectangular prism	502–505	7–9	
11A Locate, identify, and graph points on a coordinate plane and find the distance between two points	524–527, 538–544, 548–549	10–14	
11B Graph lines	528–530	15–16	
12A Divide by multiples of 10	568–569	18–19	
12B Divide and estimate quotients with 2-digit, 3-digit, and 4-digit dividends with 1- and 2-digit quotients	570–572, 574–575, 580–582, 584–585, 588–589	20–23	
10E, 11C, 12C Analyze and solve problems using skills and strategies	482–483, 494–496, 506–507, 532–533, 536–537, 546–547, 550–551	17, 24–25	

Total Test Score _____

Answer Sheet

Name _____

Test _____

1. Ⓐ Ⓑ Ⓒ Ⓓ

2. Ⓕ Ⓖ Ⓗ Ⓙ

3. Ⓐ Ⓑ Ⓒ Ⓓ

4. Ⓕ Ⓖ Ⓗ Ⓙ

5. Ⓐ Ⓑ Ⓒ Ⓓ

6. Ⓕ Ⓖ Ⓗ Ⓙ

7. Ⓐ Ⓑ Ⓒ Ⓓ

8. Ⓕ Ⓖ Ⓗ Ⓙ

9. Ⓐ Ⓑ Ⓒ Ⓓ

10. Ⓕ Ⓖ Ⓗ Ⓙ

11. Ⓐ Ⓑ Ⓒ Ⓓ

12. Ⓕ Ⓖ Ⓗ Ⓙ

13. Ⓐ Ⓑ Ⓒ Ⓓ

14. Ⓕ Ⓖ Ⓗ Ⓙ

15. Ⓐ Ⓑ Ⓒ Ⓓ

16. Ⓕ Ⓖ Ⓗ Ⓙ

17. Ⓐ Ⓑ Ⓒ Ⓓ

18. Ⓕ Ⓖ Ⓗ Ⓙ

19. Ⓐ Ⓑ Ⓒ Ⓓ

20. Ⓕ Ⓖ Ⓗ Ⓙ

21. Ⓐ Ⓑ Ⓒ Ⓓ

22. Ⓕ Ⓖ Ⓗ Ⓙ

23. Ⓐ Ⓑ Ⓒ Ⓓ

24. Ⓕ Ⓖ Ⓗ Ⓙ

25. Ⓐ Ⓑ Ⓒ Ⓓ

Answer Key

Inventory Test

Name _____ Date _____

Write the correct answer.

1. Round the number to the underlined digit.

7,562   **7,600**

2. Write the numbers in order from least to greatest.

2,834   2,384   2,482   **2,384   2,482   2,834**

3. Write the amount, using a $ sign and a decimal point.

$8.82

4. What time is it?

4:35 or four thirty-five

5. Add.   3,248
           + 1,483
           4,731

6. Subtract.   5,581
               − 2,368
               3,213

7. Find the missing measure.

6 pt = ___**3**___ qt

5

Inventory Test

Name _____ Date _____

8. Which unit would you use to measure the mass of a horse—a gram or a kilogram?

kilogram

9. Write a multiplication sentence for the array.

5 × 3 = 15

Multiply.

10. 10 × 5 = __**50**__   **11.** 6 × 4 = __**24**__   **12.** 3 × 3 × 5 = __**45**__

13. Write the special name of the figure.

isosceles triangle

14. Do the figures appear to be congruent?

__**no**__

Divide.

15. 36 ÷ 9 = __**4**__   **16.** 58 ÷ 1 = __**58**__   **17.** 27 ÷ 3 = __**9**__

18. Write the complete fact family for 7 × 4.

7 × 4 = 28   **4 × 7 = 28**   **28 ÷ 4 = 7**   **28 ÷ 7 = 4**

6

Inventory Test

Name _____ Date _____

Write the correct answer.

19. Mark the point (4, 2) on the grid.

20. Use the spinner.

Is it *certain*, *likely*, or *impossible* that the first spin will land on gray?

likely

21. Write a fraction for the shaded part.

$\frac{5}{9}$

22. Write the fractions in order from least to greatest.

$\frac{1}{4}$ $\frac{1}{3}$ $\frac{1}{6}$ $\frac{1}{6}$ $\frac{1}{4}$ $\frac{1}{3}$

23. Add.   0.65
           + 0.19
           0.84

24. Multiply.   256
               × 4
               1,024

25. Divide.   **164**
               4)656

7

Answer Key

Name _____ Date _____

Do you remember?

1. Write the number one thousand, three hundred fifty-six in standard form. __1,356__

2. Write 103 in word form. __one hundred three__

3. Write 6,594 in word form. __six thousand, five hundred ninety-four__

4. Write the value of the digit 7 in the number 7,301. __7,000__

5. Round 427 to the nearest ten. __430__

6. Round 648 to the nearest hundred. __600__

7. Round 5,809 to the nearest hundred. __5,800__

8. Round 2,513 to the nearest thousand. __3,000__

Compare. Write >, <, or = in each ◯.

9. 684 ⟨>⟩ 486

10. 921 ⟨<⟩ 927

11. 6,403 ⟨=⟩ 6,403

12. 5,172 ⟨>⟩ 4,982

Write the total value.

13. 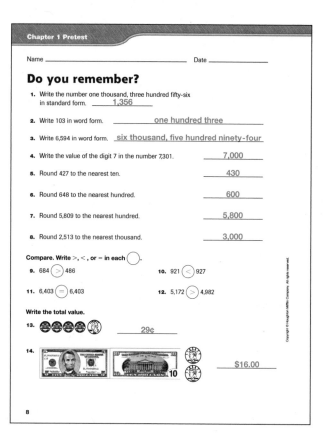 __29¢__

14. __$16.00__

8

Name _____ Date _____

Try These!

15. Write the number twenty-one thousand, eight hundred fifty in standard form. __21,850__

16. Write 16,324 in word form.

   __sixteen thousand, three hundred twenty-four__

Compare. Write >, <, or = in each ◯.

17. 168,000 ⟨>⟩ 158,000

18. 92,457 ⟨<⟩ 92,531

Round each number to the place of the underlined digit.

19. 620,499 __620,000__

20. 489,127 __500,000__

Write each number in another way.

21. 500,000 + 4,000 + 200 + 6
   __504,206; five hundred four thousand, two hundred six__

22. fourteen thousand, nine hundred eighty __14,980; 14,000 + 900 + 80__

Write the value of the underlined digit.

23. 127,413,526 __20 million__

24. 624,985,317 __600 million__

Compare. Write >, <, or = in each ◯.

25. 31,416,528 ⟨<⟩ 314,165,280

26. 1,840,920 ⟨>⟩ 1,804,920

Round each number to the place of the underlined digit.

27. 12,054,935 __12,100,000__

28. 983,097,115 __983,000,000__

9

Name _____ Date _____

Write each amount. Circle which is greater.

29. $30

$25

A $20 bill was used to buy each item below.
List the coins and bills you would use to make change.

30. cost of item: $15.55
   __2 dimes, 1 quarter, 4 $1 bills__

31. cost of item: $12.75
   __1 quarter, 2 $1 bills, 1 $5 bill__

10

Name _____ Date _____

Write the correct answers.

1. Write the expanded form of 6,340.
   __6,000 + 300 + 40__

2. Write the word form of 356.
   __three hundred fifty-six__

3. Write the word form of 9,020,000.
   __nine million, twenty thousand__

4. Write the standard form of *twenty thousand, three hundred, four.*
   __20,304__

5. Write the standard form of *six hundred thirty-six million, eighty-five thousand, forty.*
   __636,085,040__

6. What is the value of the digit 5 in 451,392?
   __50,000__

7. What is the value of the digit 8 in 528,641,037?
   __8,000,000__

Compare. Write >, <, or = in each ◯.

8. 398 ⟨>⟩ 389

9. 8,265 ⟨<⟩ 8,756

10. 435,040 ⟨=⟩ 435,040

11. 617,429,856 ⟨<⟩ 628,914,256

11

Name _____ Date _____

12. Write the numbers in order from greatest to least.

1,624   1,264   2,146

2,146   1,624   1,264

13. Write the numbers in order from least to greatest.

859,143   897,289   889,998

859,143   889,998   897,289

14. Write the numbers in order from least to greatest.

20,617,429,856   20,671,924,576   20,628,914,256

20,617,429,856   20,628,914,256   20,671,924,576

15. Round 4,712 to the nearest hundred.

4,700

16. Round 87,921 to the nearest thousand.

88,000

17. Round 4,706,427,823 to the nearest billion.

5,000,000,000

18. Which place is the number rounded to?

572,148,213 ⟶ 600,000,000

hundred million

19. Write the amount.

$1.03

Name _____ Date _____

20. Write the amount.

$45.75

21. Which is the greatest amount?

2 twenty-dollar bills and 2 five-dollar bills
1 twenty-dollar bill and 2 ten-dollar bills
3 twenty-dollar bills
4 ten-dollar bills and 2 five-dollar bills

3 twenty-dollar bills

22. A $20 bill is used to buy an item costing $16.85. Write the correct change.

1 nickel, 1 dime, 3 one dollar bills

23. Suppose 25,892 people attend a baseball game. To the nearest thousand, how many people attend the game?

26,000

24. Mark, Jayson, Andrea, and Ashley ride their bikes to school. They park their bikes side-by-side in the bike rack. Jayson's bike is next to Mark's bike. Andrea's bike is last. Mark's bike is first. In what order do the children park their bikes?

Mark, Jayson, Ashley, Andrea

25. Yolanda earns $7 for helping her neighbor plant his garden. She uses the money to buy two books. If each book costs $2.75, how much change should she get?

$1.50

Name _____ Date _____

Fill in the ◯ for the correct answer.

1. What is the expanded form of 6,340?

(A) 6 + 3 + 4
(B) 6 + 3 + 4 + 0
(C) 600 + 30 + 4
(D) **6,000 + 300 + 40**

2. What is the word form of 356?

(F) **three hundred fifty-six**
(G) three five six
(H) three hundred and fifty-six
(J) 6 hundred 35

3. What is the word form of 9,020,000?

(A) nine thousand, twenty
(B) nine million, twenty
(C) **nine million, twenty thousand**
(D) nine million, two hundred thousand

4. What is the standard form of *twenty thousand, three hundred four*?

(F) 234
(G) 20,034
(H) **20,304**
(J) 20,340

5. What is the standard form of *six hundred thirty-six million, eighty-five thousand, forty*?

(A) **636,085,040**   (B) 636,850,040   (C) 636,850,400   (D) 636,854,000

6. What is the value of the digit 5 in 451,392?

(F) 500,000
(G) **50,000**
(H) 5,000
(J) 500

7. What is the value of the digit 8 in 528,641,037?

(A) **8,000,000**   (B) 800,000
(C) 80,000   (D) 8,000

Name _____ Date _____

Choose the symbol that makes each statement true.

8. 398 ● 389

(F) **>**   (G) <   (H) =   (J) +

9. 8,265 ● 8,756

(A) >   (B) **<**   (C) =   (D) +

10. 435,040 ● 435,040

(F) >   (G) <   (H) **=**   (J) +

11. 617,429,856 ● 628,914,256

(A) >   (B) **<**   (C) =   (D) +

12. Which is in order from greatest to least?

1,624   1,264   2,146

(F) 1,264   1,624   2,146
(G) 1,624   1,264   2,146
(H) **2,146   1,624   1,264**
(J) 2,146   1,264   1,624

13. Which is in order from least to greatest?

859,143   897,289   889,998

(A) 859,143   897,289   889,998
(B) **859,143   889,998   897,289**
(C) 889,998   859,143   897,289
(D) 897,289   889,998   859,143

Answer Key

Name _____ Date _____

14. Which is in order from least to greatest?

20,617,429,856   20,671,924,576   20,628,914,256

(F) 20,617,429,856   20,628,914,256   20,671,924,576

(G) 20,617,429,856   20,671,924,756   20,628,914,256

(H) 20,628,914,256   20,617,429,856   20,671,924,756

(J) 20,671,924,756   20,628,914,256   20,617,429,856

15. Round 4,712 to the nearest hundred.

(A) 4,700   (B) 4,710   (C) 4,720   (D) 4,800

16. Round 87,921 to the nearest thousand.

(F) 87,900   (G) 87,920   (H) 88,000   (J) 89,000

17. Round 4,706,427,823 to the nearest billion.

(A) 4,000,000,000

(B) 4,707,000,000

(C) 4,708,000,000

(D) 5,000,000,000

18. Which place is the number rounded to?

572,148,213 ⟶ 600,000,000

(F) hundred millions   (G) hundred thousands

(H) millions   (J) thousands

19. Which is the amount shown?

(A) $0.90   (B) $0.93   (C) $0.98   (D) $1.03

Name _____ Date _____

20. Which is the amount shown?

(F) $40.15

(G) $45.75

(H) $50.15

(J) $50.75

21. Which is the greatest amount?

(A) 2 twenty-dollar bills and 2 five-dollar bills

(B) 1 twenty-dollar bill and 2 ten-dollar bills

(C) 3 twenty-dollar bills

(D) 4 ten-dollar bills and 2 five-dollar bills

22. A $20 bill is used to buy an item costing $16.85. Which is the correct change?

(F) 1 nickel, 1 dime, 3 one-dollar bills

(G) 1 nickel, 1 dime, 4 one-dollar bills

(H) 1 dime, 3 quarters, 4 one-dollar bills

(J) 1 dime, 3 quarters, 3 one-dollar bills

Name _____ Date _____

23. Suppose 25,892 people attend a baseball game. To the nearest thousand, how many people attend the game?

(A) 30,000

(B) 26,000

(C) 25,000

(D) 20,000

24. Mark, Jayson, Andrea, and Ashley ride their bikes to school. They park their bikes side-by-side in the bike rack. Jayson's bike is next to Mark's bike. Andrea's bike is last. Mark's bike is first. In what order do the children park their bikes?

(F) Mark, Jayson, Andrea, Ashley

(G) Mark, Ashley, Jayson, Andrea

(H) Mark, Jayson, Ashley, Andrea

(J) Mark, Ashley, Andrea, Jayson

25. Yolanda earns $7 for helping her neighbor plant his garden. She uses the money to buy two books. If each book costs $2.75, how much change should she get?

(A) $2.00

(B) $1.50

(C) $1.00

(D) $0.50

Name _____ Date _____

Do you remember?

Add or subtract.

1. 4 + 3   **7**

2. 6 + 9   **15**

3. 8 + 4   **12**

4. 7 + 9   **16**

5. 6 + 5   **11**

6. 2 + 7   **9**

7. 3 + 5   **8**

8. 9 + 8   **17**

9. 14 − 8   **6**

10. 12 − 9   **3**

11. 9 − 1   **8**

12. 14 − 9   **5**

13. 8 − 2   **6**

14. 17 − 4   **13**

15. 13 − 6   **7**

16. 19 − 10   **9**

17. 45 + 38   **83**

18. 236 − 59   **177**

19. 768 + 141   **909**

20. 537 − 285   **252**

21. 76
     + 67
     143

22. 46
     + 19
     65

23. 123
     + 599
     722

24. 456
     + 75
     531

25. 52
     − 24
     28

26. 44
     − 25
     19

27. 311
     − 199
     112

28. 675
     − 598
     77

Name _____ Date _____

Try These!

Complete each number sentence. Tell which property of addition you used.

29. $32 + 56 =$ __56__ $+ 32$ _____Commutative_____

30. $(15 + 6) + 7 = 15 + (6 +$ __7__ $)$ _____Associative_____

31. $999 + 0 =$ __999__ _____Zero Property For Addition_____

Add or subtract.

32.	**33.**	**34.**	**35.**
1,146 + 876 **2,022**	2,397 + 1,439 **3,836**	2,447 + 556 **3,003**	8,392 + 177 **8,569**
36.	**37.**	**38.**	**39.**
1,817 + 993 **2,810**	3,912 + 1,487 **5,399**	2,333 + 5,678 **8,011**	7,227 + 8,349 **15,576**
40.	**41.**	**42.**	**43.**
1,246 − 347 **899**	5,231 − 3,863 **1,368**	34,721 − 29,719 **5,002**	24,322 − 17,853 **6,469**
44.	**45.**	**46.**	**47.**
40,000 − 30,941 **9,059**	10,400 − 8,231 **2,169**	12,500 − 12,098 **402**	3,006 − 239 **2,767**

Round each number to the nearest hundred. Estimate the sum or difference.

48.	**49.**
6,893 + 542 **7,400**	4,251 − 1,294 **3,000**
50.	**51.**
25,989 + 36,146 **62,100**	8,973 − 2,613 **6,400**

20

Name _____ Date _____

Write the correct answer for each.

1. Group or rearrange the addends so that you can add mentally. Then find the sum.

$234 + 492 + 8$ _____734_____

2. Complete the number sentence. Which property of addition did you use?

$14 + 37 =$ _____ $+ 14$ _____37; commutative_____

3.	**4.**	**5.**
456 + 235 **691**	979 + 1,112 **2,091**	16,982 + 24,218 **41,200**
6.	**7.**	**8.**
532 − 186 **346**	12,917 − 3,828 **9,089**	2,563 − 275 **2,288**

9. Round each number to the nearest ten. Then estimate.

$487 + 316 =$ _____810_____

10. Round each number to the nearest dollar. Then estimate.

$83.25 − $15.99 =$ _____$67_____

11. Round each to the nearest hundred. Then estimate.

$4,075 + 750 =$ _____4,900_____

12.	**13.**	**14.**
103 − 87 **16**	35,000 − 4,010 **30,990**	5,004 − 971 **4,033**

15. Simplify the expression.

$(14 + 2) + (24 − 9)$ _____31_____

21

Name _____ Date _____

16. Complete by choosing >, <, or = .

$7 + (112 − 19)$ $\bigcirc{=}$ $(112 − 19) + 7$

17. Evaluate the expression when $x = 6$.

$x + 5$ _____11_____

18. Evaluate the expression when $n = 8$.

$(n − 3) + 2$ _____7_____

19. Solve the equation.

$r + 4 = 12$ _____8_____

20. Solve the equation.

$t − 3 = 10$ _____13_____

21. Find the value of y for the following equation when $x = 5$.

$y = x + 2$ _____7_____

22. Find the value of n for the following equation when $m = 12$.

$n = m − 10$ _____2_____

23. Pedro bought a turkey wrap for $3.75 and a small fruit juice for $1.55. About how much change should he get back from a $20 bill? _____$14_____

24. The normal monthly temperature in June in Portland, Oregon, is 16° cooler than the normal monthly temperature in June in Mobile, Alabama. The normal monthly temperature in June in Mobile, Alabama, is 80°F. What is the normal monthly temperature in June in Portland? _____64°_____

25. Together, Madie and Beth have 48 CDs. Beth has 8 more CDs than Madie. How many CDs does Madie have? _____20_____

22

Name _____ Date _____

Fill in the ○ for the correct answer.

1. Group or rearrange the addends so that you can add mentally. Then find the sum.

$234 + 492 + 8$

(A) 534   (B) 634
(C) 734   (D) 834

2. Complete the number sentence. Which property of addition did you use?

$14 + 37 =$ ▓ $+ 14$

(F) 37; Associative   **(G) 37; Commutative**
(H) 37; Zero property   (J) 14; Commutative

3. 456 + 235	**4.** 979 + 1,112	**5.** 16,982 + 24,218
(A) 681 **(B) 691** (C) 781 (D) 791	**(F) 2,091** (G) 2,081 (H) 1,091 (J) 1,081	(A) 30,190 (B) 32,200 (C) 40,200 **(D) 41,200**
6. 532 − 186	**7.** 12,917 − 3,828	**8.** 2,563 − 275
(F) 456 (G) 445 **(H) 346** (J) 345	(A) 11,111 (B) 9,111 (C) 9,099 **(D) 9,089**	(F) 2,312 **(G) 2,288** (H) 2,212 (J) 288

9. Round each number to the nearest ten. Then estimate.

$487 + 316 =$

(A) 810   (B) 800   (C) 790   (D) 700

23

Answer Key

Name _____ Date _____

10. Round each number to the nearest dollar. Then estimate.

$83.25 - $15.99 =

(F) $60   (G) $64   (H) $67   (J) $68

11. Round each to the nearest hundred. Then estimate.

4,075 + 750 =

(A) 4,700   (B) 4,800   (C) 4,900   (D) 5,000

12. 103
        − 87

(F) 26
(G) 24
(H) 16
(J) 6

13. 35,000
        − 4,010

(A) 30,010
(B) 30,990
(C) 31,010
(D) 31,990

14. 5,004
        − 971

(F) 4,033
(G) 4,037
(H) 4,937
(J) 4,973

15. Simplify the expression.

(14 + 2) + (24 − 9)

(A) 31   (B) 29
(D) 19   (C) 21

16. Complete by choosing >, <, or =.

7 + (112 − 19) ◯ (112 − 19) + 7

(F) >   (G) <   (H) =

17. Evaluate the expression when $x = 6$.

$x + 5$

(A) 1   (B) 2
(C) 11   (D) 12

18. Evaluate the expression when $n = 8$.

$(n − 3) + 2$

(F) 3   (G) 7
(H) 9   (J) 13

24

Name _____ Date _____

19. Solve the equation.

$r + 4 = 12$

(A) 3   (B) 8
(C) 16   (D) 48

20. Solve the equation.

$t − 3 = 10$

(F) 13   (G) 10
(H) 7   (J) 3

21. Find the value of y for the following equation when $x = 5$.

$y = x + 2$

(A) 2   (B) 5   (C) 7   (D) 10

22. Find the value of n for the following equation when $m = 12$.

$n = m − 10$

(F) 22   (G) 12   (H) 8   (J) 2

23. Pedro bought a turkey wrap for $3.75 and a small fruit juice for $1.55. About how much change should he get back from a $20 bill?

(A) $16   (B) $14   (C) $6   (D) $4

24. The normal monthly temperature in June in Portland, Oregon, is 16° cooler than the normal monthly temperature in June in Mobile, Alabama. The normal monthly temperature in June in Mobile, Alabama, is 80°F. What is the normal monthly temperature in June in Portland?

(F) 96°F   (G) 76°F   (H) 74°F   (J) 64°F

25. Together, Madie and Beth have 48 CDs. Beth has 8 more CDs than Madie. How many CDs does Madie have?

(A) 20   (B) 28   (C) 32   (D) 40

25

Name _____ Date _____

Do you remember?

Multiply.

1. 6 × 3 ___18___

2. 5 × 5 ___25___

3. 9 × 6 ___54___

4. 3 × 8 ___24___

5. 7 × 5 ___35___

Divide.

6. 16 ÷ 4 ___4___

7. 27 ÷ 3 ___9___

8. 42 ÷ 7 ___6___

9. 81 ÷ 9 ___9___

10. 36 ÷ 4 ___9___

Try These!

Find each product.
Use double facts to help you.

11. 8 × 4 ___32___

12. 6 × 5 ___30___

26

Name _____ Date _____

Solve each equation.
Name the property you used.

13. $1 × 45 = n$ ___45; Property of One___

14. $(4 × 3) × 8 = 4 × (n × 8)$ ___3; Associative Property___

Find each product.

15. 10 × 8 ___80___

16. 9 × 8 ___72___

17. 7 × 9 ___63___

Find each quotient.

18. 24 ÷ 4 ___6___

19. 36 ÷ 6 ___6___

20. 42 ÷ 7 ___6___

21. 45 ÷ 9 ___5___

22. 18 ÷ 4 ___4 R2___

23. 53 ÷ 7 ___7 R4___

Solve.
If an equation has no solution, tell why.

24. $30 ÷ 7 = n$ ___4 R2___

25. $51 ÷ 8 = n$ ___6 R3___

26. $27 ÷ 1 = n$ ___27___

27. $5 ÷ 0 = n$ ___no solution; cannot divide by 0___

27

Name _____ Date _____

Write the correct answer.

Find each product. Use double facts to help you.

1. $5 \times 10 =$ __50__

2. $8 \times 6 =$ __48__

Find each product.

3. $3 \times 9 =$ __27__

4. $7 \times 5 =$ __35__

5. $8 \times 7 =$ __56__

6. $6 \times 6 =$ __36__

7. Write the fact family for the set of numbers 7, 6, and 42.

__$7 \times 6 = 42$__   __$6 \times 7 = 42$__

__$42 \div 6 = 7$__   __$42 \div 7 = 6$__

Find each quotient.

8. $32 \div 8 =$ __4__

9. $24 \div 6 =$ __4__

10. $21 \div 3 =$ __7__

11. $45 \div 5 =$ __9__

Find each quotient and remainder.

12. $35 \div 8 =$ __4 R3__

13. $25 \div 4 =$ __6 R1__

Solve each equation. Name the property that you used.

14. $7 \times 3 = 3 \times m$ __7; Commutative Property__

15. $(3 \times 6) \times 5 = w \times (6 \times 5)$ __3; Associative Property__

28

Name _____ Date _____

Solve.

16. $n \div 9 = 1$ __9__

17. $18 \div 0 = d$ __not possible__

Evaluate each expression when $n = 5$.

18. $3n$ __15__

19. $8n - 2$ __38__

Evaluate each expression when $a = 3$.

20. $18 \div a$ __6__

21. $3 + 2a$ __9__

Solve each equation.

22. $4a = 16$ __4__

23. $7 = 14 \div m$ __2__

24. Mike is collecting bugs for a science project. Mike has collected 9 bugs. Amy wants to collect three times as many bugs as Mike. How many bugs must Amy collect?

__27__

25. Pamela can buy one pen for $2 or 4 pens for $5. How much will she pay for 5 pens?

__$7__

29

Name _____ Date _____

Fill in the ◯ for the correct answer.

Find each product. Use double facts to help you.

1. $5 \times 10 =$ (A) 50   (B) 15   (C) 5   (D) 2

2. $8 \times 6 =$ (F) 14   (G) 24   (H) 36   (J) 48

Find each product.

3. $3 \times 9 =$ (A) 12   (B) 18   (C) 27   (D) 36

4. $7 \times 5 =$ (F) 42   (G) 35   (H) 28   (J) 21

5. $8 \times 7 =$ (A) 15   (B) 36   (C) 48   (D) 56

6. $6 \times 6 =$ (F) 12   (G) 24   (H) 36   (J) 42

7. Find the fact family for the set of numbers 7, 6, and 42.

(A) $7 \times 6 = 42$ $6 \times 7 = 42$ $42 \div 6 = 7$ $42 \div 7 = 6$

(B) $42 \times 6 = 7$ $42 \times 7 = 6$ $42 \div 6 = 7$ $42 \div 7 = 6$

(C) $6 \times 7 = 42$ $42 \times 6 = 7$ $42 \div 7 = 6$ $7 \div 6 = 42$

(D) $42 \times 7 = 6$ $7 \times 6 = 42$ $6 \div 42 = 7$ $7 \div 6 = 42$

Find each quotient.

8. $32 \div 8 =$ (F) 16   (G) 8   (H) 4   (J) 2

9. $24 \div 6 =$ (A) 2   (B) 4   (C) 8   (D) 12

10. $21 \div 3 =$ (F) 7   (G) 14   (H) 21   (J) 63

11. $45 \div 5 =$ (A) 9   (B) 8   (C) 7   (D) 6

Find each quotient and remainder.

12. $35 \div 8 =$ (F) 5 R5   (G) 4 R3   (H) 3 R4   (J) 3 R3

13. $25 \div 4 =$ (A) 6 R1   (B) 5 R5   (C) 5 R1   (D) 4 R1

30

Name _____ Date _____

Solve each equation. Name the property that you used.

14. $7 \times 3 = 3 \times m$ (F) 7; Associative Property   (G) 7; Commutative Property   (H) 3; Associative Property   (J) 3; Commutative Property

15. $(3 \times 6) \times 5 = w \times (6 \times 5)$ (A) 3; Associative Property   (B) 5; Associative Property   (C) 6; Associative Property   (D) 3; Commutative Property

Solve.

16. $n \div 9 = 1$ (F) 0   (G) 1   (H) 9   (J) not possible

17. $18 \div 0 = d$ (A) 0   (B) 1   (C) 18   (D) not possible

Evaluate each expression when $n = 5$.

18. $3n$ (F) 3   (G) 5   (H) 8   (J) 15

19. $8n - 2$ (A) 38   (B) 20   (C) 11   (D) 9

Evaluate each expression when $a = 3$.

20. $18 \div a$ (F) 21   (G) 15   (H) 9   (J) 6

21. $3 + 2a$ (A) 8   (B) 9   (C) 11   (D) 13

Solve each equation.

22. $4a = 16$ (F) 12   (G) 8   (H) 4   (J) 2

23. $7 = 14 \div m$ (A) 2   (B) 7   (C) 14   (D) 28

24. Mike is collecting bugs for a science project. Mike has collected 9 bugs. Amy wants to collect three times as many bugs as Mike. How many bugs must Amy collect?

(F) 6   (G) 9   (H) 12   (J) 27

25. Pamela can buy one pen for $2 or 4 pens for $5. How much will she pay for 5 pens?

(A) $4   (B) $5   (C) $7   (D) $10

31

Answer Key

Name _____ Date _____

Find each product.

1. 8×8 __64__

2. 3×8 __24__

3. 4×7 __28__

4. 7×7 __49__

Solve each equation. Name the property you used.

5. $6 \times 8 = n \times 6$ __8; Commutative__

6. $(3 \times 7) \times 2 = n \times (7 \times 2)$ __3; Associative__

7. $3 \times n = 3$ __1; Property of One__

8. $8 \times n = 0$ __0; Zero Property__

Round to the greatest place.

9. 22 __20__

10. 364 __400__

11. 652 __700__

12. 4,468 __4,000__

Try These!

Use basic facts and patterns to find each product.

13. 6×4 __24__

6×40 __240__

14. 5×70 __350__

5×700 __3,500__

Find each product.

15.
$$\begin{array}{r} 79 \\ \times\ 7 \\ \hline 553 \end{array}$$

16.
$$\begin{array}{r} 82 \\ \times\ 6 \\ \hline 492 \end{array}$$

32

Name _____ Date _____

17.
$$\begin{array}{r} 368 \\ \times\ 4 \\ \hline 1,472 \end{array}$$

18.
$$\begin{array}{r} 792 \\ \times\ 5 \\ \hline 3,960 \end{array}$$

19.
$$\begin{array}{r} 6,192 \\ \times\ 3 \\ \hline 18,576 \end{array}$$

20.
$$\begin{array}{r} 8,964 \\ \times\ 6 \\ \hline 53,784 \end{array}$$

21. 204×8 __1,632__

22. $5,006 \times 7$ __35,042__

23. 8×60 __480__

24. 50×400 __20,000__

25. 46×21 __966__

26. 83×95 __7,885__

27. 846×27 __22,842__

28. 340×38 __12,920__

Estimate each product.

29. $\$3.84 \times 6$ __\$24.00__

30. 469×7 __3,500__

33

Name _____ Date _____

Write the correct answer.

Use basic facts and patterns to find each product.

1. $3 \times 70 = $ __210__

2. $6 \times 400 = $ __2,400__

3. $8 \times 9,000 = $ __72,000__

Find each product.

4.
$$\begin{array}{r} 43 \\ \times\ 6 \\ \hline 258 \end{array}$$

5.
$$\begin{array}{r} 86 \\ \times\ 5 \\ \hline 430 \end{array}$$

6.
$$\begin{array}{r} 72 \\ \times\ 9 \\ \hline 648 \end{array}$$

7.
$$\begin{array}{r} 642 \\ \times\ 7 \\ \hline 4,494 \end{array}$$

8. $3 \times \$8.46 = $ __\$25.38__

9.
$$\begin{array}{r} 495 \\ \times\ 6 \\ \hline 2,970 \end{array}$$

10.
$$\begin{array}{r} 3,894 \\ \times\ 8 \\ \hline 31,152 \end{array}$$

11. $2 \times 4,663 = $ __9,326__

12. $9 \times 209 = $ __1,881__

13. $4 \times 3,008 = $ __12,032__

14. $7 \times 7,300 = $ __51,100__

Estimate each product.

15.
$$\begin{array}{r} 65 \\ \times\ 4 \\ \hline 280 \end{array}$$

16.
$$\begin{array}{r} 788 \\ \times\ 5 \\ \hline 4,000 \end{array}$$

17.
$$\begin{array}{r} 3,289 \\ \times\ 6 \\ \hline 18,000 \end{array}$$

34

Name _____ Date _____

Multiply.

18.
$$\begin{array}{r} 40 \\ \times\ 30 \\ \hline 1,200 \end{array}$$

19.
$$\begin{array}{r} 800 \\ \times\ 70 \\ \hline 56,000 \end{array}$$

20.
$$\begin{array}{r} 36 \\ \times\ 24 \\ \hline 864 \end{array}$$

21. $65 \times 83 = $ __5,395__

22. $489 \times 29 = $ __14,181__

Solve.

23. Jon built 6 towers with blocks. The smallest was 4 blocks high, the next was 7 blocks high, and the third was 10 blocks high. If he continues this pattern, how many blocks high will the tallest tower be?

__19__

24. Bobby has a car collection. He has 24 cars displayed on each of 4 shelves. How many cars does he have in his collection?

__96__

25. The students at Oak Crest Elementary School raised money to donate to a local charity. If students in the fourth grade raised 3 times the amount of money students in the third grade raised, how much did the fourth grade raise?

Money Raised	
First Grade	$ $ $
Second Grade	$ $
Third Grade	$ $ $ $
Fourth Grade	
Fifth Grade	$ $ $ $ $

Each $ = $20.00

__240__

35

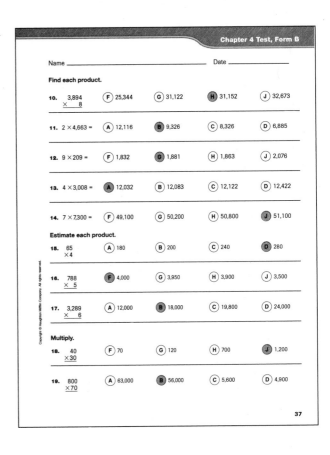

Chapter 4 Test, Form B

Name _____ Date _____

Fill in the ◯ for the correct answer.

Use basic facts and patterns to find each product.

1. 3 × 70 = (A) 180 **(B) 210** (C) 240 (D) 2,100

2. 6 × 400 = (F) 240 (G) 1,800 **(H) 2,400** (J) 30,000

3. 8 × 9,000 = (A) 7,000 (B) 64,000 **(C) 72,000** (D) 74,000

Find each product.

4. 43 × 6 (F) 2,418 **(G) 258** (H) 249 (J) 198

5. 86 × 5 **(A) 430** (B) 1,330 (C) 4,011 (D) 4,030

6. 72 × 9 (F) 631 (G) 638 **(H) 648** (J) 711

7. 642 × 7 (A) 44,814 **(B) 4,494** (C) 4,484 (D) 4,294

8. 3 × $8.46 = (F) $24.38 **(G) $25.38** (H) $26.01 (J) $252.18

9. 495 × 6 (A) 2,470 (B) 2,940 **(C) 2,970** (D) 2,943

36

Chapter 4 Test, Form B

Name _____ Date _____

Find each product.

10. 3,894 × 8 (F) 25,344 (G) 31,122 **(H) 31,152** (J) 32,673

11. 2 × 4,663 = (A) 12,116 (B) 9,326 (C) 8,326 (D) 6,885

12. 9 × 209 = (F) 1,832 **(G) 1,881** (H) 1,863 (J) 2,076

13. 4 × 3,008 = **(A) 12,032** (B) 12,083 (C) 12,122 (D) 12,422

14. 7 × 7,300 = (F) 49,100 (G) 50,200 (H) 50,800 **(J) 51,100**

Estimate each product.

15. 65 × 4 (A) 180 (B) 200 (C) 240 **(D) 280**

16. 788 × 5 **(F) 4,000** (G) 3,950 (H) 3,900 (J) 3,500

17. 3,289 × 6 (A) 12,000 **(B) 18,000** (C) 19,800 (D) 24,000

Multiply.

18. 40 × 30 (F) 70 (G) 120 (H) 700 **(J) 1,200**

19. 800 × 70 (A) 63,000 **(B) 56,000** (C) 5,600 (D) 4,900

37

Chapter 4 Test, Form B

Name _____ Date _____

Multiply.

20. 36 × 24 (F) 210 (G) 216 **(H) 864** (J) 882

21. 65 × 83 = (A) 715 (B) 5,025 (C) 5,095 **(D) 5,395**

22. 489 × 29 = (F) 5,379 (G) 13,758 **(H) 14,181** (J) 20,881

23. Jon built 6 towers with blocks. The smallest was 4 blocks high, the next was 7 blocks high, and the third was 10 blocks high. If he continues this pattern, how many blocks high will the tallest tower be?

(A) 16 **(B) 19** (C) 21 (D) 27

24. Bobby has a car collection. He has 24 cars displayed on each of 4 shelves. How many cars does he have in his collection?

(F) 6 (G) 20 (H) 28 **(J) 96**

25. The students at Oak Crest Elementary School raised money to donate to a local charity. If students in the fourth grade raised 3 times the amount of money students in the third grade raised, how much did the fourth grade raise?

Money Raised	
First Grade	$ $ $
Second Grade	$ $
Third Grade	$ $ $ $
Fourth Grade	
Fifth Grade	$ $ $ $ $

Each $ = $20.00

(A) $240 (B) $80 (C) $60 (D) $12

38

Chapter 5 Pretest

Name _____ Date _____

Do you remember?

1. 3 + 4 = __7__   2. 8 + 2 = __10__

3. 7 + 6 = __13__   4. 9 + 8 = __17__

5. 6 − 4 = __2__   6. 11 − 5 = __6__

7. 14 − 8 = __6__   8. 16 − 9 = __7__

9. 3 × 7 = __21__   10. 4 × 8 = __32__

11. 6 × 7 = __42__   12. 7 × 8 = __56__

13. 54 ÷ 9 = __6__   14. 48 ÷ 6 = __8__

15. 28 ÷ 7 = __4__   16. 72 ÷ 8 = __9__

17. 4)̅3̅7̅ **9 R1**   18. 7)̅2̅4̅ **3 R3**

19. 8)̅6̅6̅ **8 R2**   20. 6)̅3̅4̅ **5 R4**

39

Answer Key

Chapter 5 Pretest

Name _____ Date _____

Write all the factors of each number.

21. 12   _1, 2, 3, 4, 6, 12_   22. 15   _1, 3, 5, 15_

Try These!

Divide

23. 4)46   11 R2   24. 2)44   22

25. 5)65   13   26. 7)99   14 R1

27. 3)300   100   28. 5)5,000   1000

29. 3)396   132   30. 5)606   121 R1

31. 6)496   82 R4   32. 8)656   82

33. 4)$0.72 $0.18   34. 5)$8.05 $1.61

35. 2)413   206 R1   36. 3)627   209

40

Chapter 5 Test, Form A

Name _____ Date _____

Write the correct answer.

Divide.

1. 4)44   11

2. 4)35   8 R3

3. 6)83   13 R5

4. 6,400 ÷ 8 =   800

5. 143 ÷ 7 =   20 R3

6. 8)$7.60 $0.95

7. 4)160   40

8. 520 ÷ 5 =   104

9. 5)605   121

Estimate.

10. 29 ÷ 4 =   7   11. 48 ÷ 9 =   5

12. 219 ÷ 7 =   30   13. 553 ÷ 5 =   110

Divide.

14. 8)1,368   171   15. 4)20,020   5,005

16. 1,925 ÷ 5 =   385   17. 10,080 ÷ 8 =   1,260

41

Chapter 5 Test, Form A

Name _____ Date _____

18. Which numbers are divisible by 2, 5, and 10?   _20_

    15, 20, 25, 35

19. Which number is prime?   _17_

    4, 9, 15, 17

20. Which number is composite?   _4_

    2, 4, 7, 19

21. Which list contains only prime numbers?   _11, 17, 19, 23_

    2, 5, 9, 12

    2, 7, 17, 27

    10, 15, 17, 19

    11, 17, 19, 23

Find the average of the numbers in each group.

22. 63, 19, 17, 13   _28_

23. 126, 134, 238   _166_

24. Len is donating 28 pencils for his class supply box. If pencils are sold in packages of 8, how many packages does Len need to buy?

    _4_

25. Rosa sold 2 more candy bars than Ricky. Ricky sold 3 fewer candy bars than Rachael. Rachael sold twice as many candy bars as Rita. If Rita sold 15 candy bars, how many did Rosa sell?

    _29_

42

Chapter 5 Test, Form B

Name _____ Date _____

Fill in the ◯ for the correct answer.

Divide.

1. 4)44   Ⓐ 12   Ⓑ 11   Ⓒ 11   Ⓓ 10

2. 4)35   Ⓕ 7 R7   Ⓖ 8   Ⓗ 8 R3   Ⓙ 9

3. 6)83   Ⓐ 21   Ⓑ 13 R5   Ⓒ 13   Ⓓ 12

4. 6,400 ÷ 8 = ▩   Ⓕ 80   Ⓖ 720   Ⓗ 800   Ⓙ 8,000

5. 143 ÷ 7 = ▩   Ⓐ 20   Ⓑ 20 R3   Ⓒ 21 R3   Ⓓ 23

6. 8)$7.60   Ⓕ $0.90   Ⓖ $0.92   Ⓗ $0.93   Ⓙ $0.95

7. 4)160   Ⓐ 4   Ⓑ 38   Ⓒ 38 R8   Ⓓ 40

8. 520 ÷ 5 = ▩   Ⓕ 104   Ⓖ 130   Ⓗ 84   Ⓙ 72

9. 5)605   Ⓐ 12 R5   Ⓑ 120   Ⓒ 120 R5   Ⓓ 121

43

144

Name _____ Date _____

Estimate.

10. 29 ÷ 4 = ▨   (F) 5   (G) 6   (H) 7   (J) 8

11. 48 ÷ 9 = ▨   (A) 4   (B) 5   (C) 6   (D) 7

12. 219 ÷ 7 = ▨   (F) 20   (G) 30   (H) 35   (J) 40

13. 553 ÷ 5 = ▨   (A) 90   (B) 100   (C) 110   (D) 120

Divide.

14. 8)‾1,368   (F) 171   (G) 168   (H) 161   (J) 158

15. 4)‾20,020   (A) 4,005   (B) 5,000   (C) 5,004   (D) 5,005

16. 1,925 ÷ 5 = ▨   (F) 385   (G) 381   (H) 380   (J) 305

17. 10,080 ÷ 8 = ▨   (A) 1,210   (B) 1,259   (C) 1,260   (D) 1,261

18. Which number is divisible by 2, 5, and 10?
(F) 15   (G) 20   (H) 25   (J) all of these

19. Which number is prime?
(A) 17   (B) 15   (C) 9   (D) 4

44

Name _____ Date _____

20. Which number is composite?
(F) 19   (G) 7   (H) 4   (J) 2

21. Which list contains only prime numbers?
(A) 2, 5, 9, 12   (B) 2, 7, 17, 27   (C) 10, 15, 17, 19   (D) 11, 17, 19, 23

Find the average of the numbers in each group.

22. 63, 19, 17, 13
(F) 28   (G) 30   (H) 32   (J) 40

23. 126, 134, 238
(A) 125   (B) 166   (C) 249   (D) 498

24. Len is donating 28 pencils for his class supply box. If pencils are sold in packages of 8, how many packages does Len need to buy?
(F) 3   (G) 4   (H) 5   (J) 6

25. Rosa sold 2 more candy bars than Ricky. Ricky sold 3 fewer candy bars than Rachael. Rachael sold twice as many candy bars as Rita. If Rita sold 15 candy bars, how many did Rosa sell?
(A) 32   (B) 30   (C) 29   (D) 28

45

Name _____ Date _____

Do you remember?

Measure each line segment to the nearest inch or half inch.

1. •——•   1 inch

2. •————————•   3 inches

3. •——————•   2 ½ inches

4. Measure to the nearest centimeter.
•————•   3 cm

Answer each question about capacity.

5. Which unit would you use to measure the capacity of a water pitcher, cups or gallons?   cups

6. Which unit would you use to measure the capacity of a bathtub, pints or gallons?   gallons

7. 1 liter = ___1,000___ milliliters

8. 3,000 milliliters = ___3___ liters

Answer each question about weight or mass.

9. Which unit would you use to measure the weight of a large dog, ounces or pounds?   pounds

10. Which unit would you use to measure the mass of a box of cereal, grams or kilograms?   grams

11. 1 kilogram = ___1,000___ grams

12. 4,000 grams = ___4___ kilograms

46

Name _____ Date _____

What time is shown?

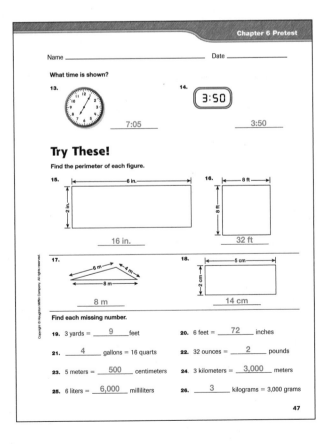

13. 7:05

14. 3:50 — 3:50

Try These!

Find the perimeter of each figure.

15. 6 in. × 2 in.   16 in.

16. 8 ft × 8 ft   32 ft

17. 6 m, 4 m, 8 m   8 m

18. 5 cm × 2 cm   14 cm

Find each missing number.

19. 3 yards = ___9___ feet

20. 6 feet = ___72___ inches

21. ___4___ gallons = 16 quarts

22. 32 ounces = ___2___ pounds

23. 5 meters = ___500___ centimeters

24. 3 kilometers = ___3,000___ meters

25. 6 liters = ___6,000___ milliliters

26. ___3___ kilograms = 3,000 grams

47

Answer Key

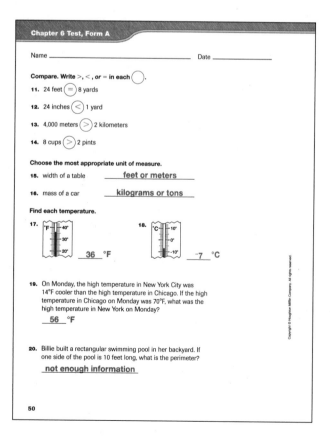

Chapter 6 Pretest

Name _____ Date _____

Write each temperature.

27. 44°F
28. −5°F
29. 10°C
30. −8°C

48

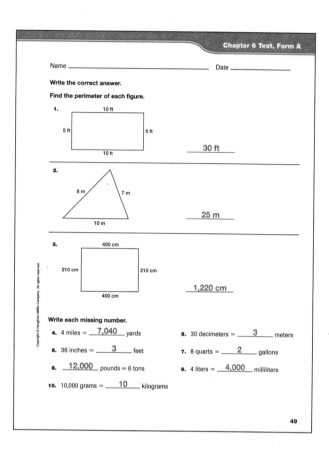

Chapter 6 Test, Form A

Name _____ Date _____

Write the correct answer.

Find the perimeter of each figure.

1. 10 ft, 5 ft, 5 ft, 10 ft — **30 ft**

2. 8 m, 7 m, 10 m — **25 m**

3. 400 cm, 210 cm, 210 cm, 400 cm — **1,220 cm**

Write each missing number.

4. 4 miles = __7,040__ yards
5. 30 decimeters = __3__ meters
6. 36 inches = __3__ feet
7. 8 quarts = __2__ gallons
8. __12,000__ pounds = 6 tons
9. 4 liters = __4,000__ milliliters
10. 10,000 grams = __10__ kilograms

49

Chapter 6 Test, Form A

Name _____ Date _____

Compare. Write >, <, or = in each ◯.

11. 24 feet ⊜ 8 yards
12. 24 inches ⊖< 1 yard
13. 4,000 meters ⊖> 2 kilometers
14. 8 cups ⊖> 2 pints

Choose the most appropriate unit of measure.

15. width of a table   **feet or meters**

16. mass of a car   **kilograms or tons**

Find each temperature.

17. **36** °F
18. **−7** °C

19. On Monday, the high temperature in New York City was 14°F cooler than the high temperature in Chicago. If the high temperature in Chicago on Monday was 70°F, what was the high temperature in New York on Monday?

    56 °F

20. Billie built a rectangular swimming pool in her backyard. If one side of the pool is 10 feet long, what is the perimeter?

    not enough information

50

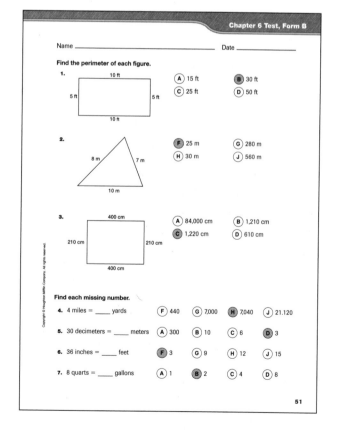

Chapter 6 Test, Form B

Name _____ Date _____

Find the perimeter of each figure.

1. 10 ft, 5 ft, 5 ft, 10 ft
   - (A) 15 ft
   - **(B) 30 ft**
   - (C) 25 ft
   - (D) 50 ft

2. 8 m, 7 m, 10 m
   - (F) 25 m
   - (G) 280 m
   - **(H) 30 m**
   - (J) 560 m

3. 400 cm, 210 cm, 210 cm, 400 cm
   - (A) 84,000 cm
   - (B) 1,210 cm
   - **(C) 1,220 cm**
   - (D) 610 cm

Find each missing number.

4. 4 miles = ____ yards
   - (F) 440
   - (G) 7,000
   - **(H) 7,040**
   - (J) 21.120

5. 30 decimeters = ____ meters
   - (A) 300
   - (B) 10
   - (C) 6
   - **(D) 3**

6. 36 inches = ____ feet
   - **(F) 3**
   - (G) 9
   - (H) 12
   - (J) 15

7. 8 quarts = ____ gallons
   - (A) 1
   - **(B) 2**
   - (C) 4
   - (D) 8

51

Chapter 6 Test, Form B

Name _____ Date _____

Find each missing number.

8. _____ pounds = 6 tons

   (F) 18,000 (G) 12,000 (H) 6,000 (J) 1,200

9. 4 liters = _____ milliliters

   (A) 40 (B) 400 (C) 4,000 (D) 8,000

10. 10,000 grams = _____ kilograms

   (F) 1 (G) 10 (H) 20 (J) 100

Which symbol makes each statement true?

11. 24 feet ● 8 yards
   (A) > (B) <
   (C) = (D) +

12. 24 inches ● 1 yard
   (F) > (G) <
   (H) = (J) +

13. 4,000 meters ● 2 kilometers
   (A) > (B) <
   (C) = (D) +

14. 8 cups ● 2 pints
   (F) > (G) <
   (H) = (J) +

Choose the most appropriate unit of measure.

15. width of a table
   (A) inches (B) feet
   (C) yards (D) miles

16. mass of a car
   (F) kilograms (G) milligrams
   (H) grams (J) ounces

52

Chapter 6 Test, Form B

Name _____ Date _____

Find each temperature.

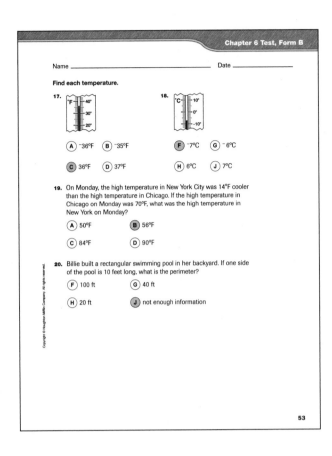

17. (A) ⁻36°F (B) ⁻35°F
    (C) 36°F (D) 37°F

18. (F) ⁻7°C (G) ⁻6°C
    (H) 6°C (J) 7°C

19. On Monday, the high temperature in New York City was 14°F cooler than the high temperature in Chicago. If the high temperature in Chicago on Monday was 70°F, what was the high temperature in New York on Monday?

    (A) 50°F (B) 56°F
    (C) 84°F (D) 90°F

20. Billie built a rectangular swimming pool in her backyard. If one side of the pool is 10 feet long, what is the perimeter?

    (F) 100 ft (G) 40 ft
    (H) 20 ft (J) not enough information

53

Chapter 7 Pretest

Name _____ Date _____

Do you remember?

Write a fraction for the shaded part.

1. $\frac{1}{3}$

2. $\frac{1}{4}$

Write a fraction for the shaded part.

3. $\frac{1}{5}$

4. $\frac{3}{4}$

Compare. Write >, <, or = in each ○.

5. $\frac{1}{2}$ (>) $\frac{1}{3}$

6. $\frac{1}{8}$ (=) $\frac{1}{8}$

7. $\frac{1}{9}$ (<) $\frac{1}{4}$

8. $\frac{1}{5}$ (>) $\frac{1}{6}$

Write yes or no to tell whether each pair of fractions is equivalent.

9. $\frac{2}{3}$ and $\frac{4}{6}$ yes

10. $\frac{1}{4}$ and $\frac{3}{8}$ no

11. $\frac{3}{5}$ and $\frac{6}{10}$ yes

12. $\frac{5}{6}$ and $\frac{1}{3}$ no

Try These!

Write the fraction for the shaded part.

13. $\frac{3}{8}$

14. $\frac{7}{12}$

54

Chapter 7 Pretest

Name _____ Date _____

Find the fractional part of each number.

15. $\frac{1}{3}$ of 9   3

16. $\frac{1}{2}$ of 16   8

17. $\frac{3}{4}$ of 8   6

18. $\frac{2}{3}$ of 12   8

Write each fraction in simplest form.

19. $\frac{9}{12}$ $\frac{3}{4}$

20. $\frac{10}{15}$ $\frac{2}{3}$

Compare. Write >, <, or = in each ○.

21. $\frac{4}{9}$ (>) $\frac{2}{9}$

22. $\frac{2}{3}$ (<) $\frac{5}{6}$

23. Write a mixed number for $\frac{8}{3}$. $2\frac{2}{3}$

24. Write an improper fraction for $3\frac{3}{4}$. $\frac{15}{4}$

Add or subtract. Write each sum or difference in simplest form.

25. $\frac{4}{6} + \frac{1}{6}$ $\frac{5}{6}$

26. $\frac{5}{9} + \frac{3}{9}$ $\frac{8}{9}$

27. $2\frac{3}{7} + 4\frac{3}{7}$ $6\frac{6}{7}$

28. $4\frac{1}{3} + 3\frac{2}{3}$ 8

29. $\frac{9}{10} - \frac{5}{10}$ $\frac{2}{5}$

30. $\frac{4}{5} - \frac{2}{5}$ $\frac{2}{5}$

31. $8\frac{3}{4} - 6\frac{3}{4}$ 2

32. $7\frac{4}{7} - 2\frac{3}{7}$ $5\frac{1}{7}$

55

147

Answer Key

Name _____ Date _____

Write the correct answer.

1. Write the fraction for the shaded part.
□ □ ▨ ▨ ▨ $\frac{3}{5}$

Find the fractional part of each number.

2. $\frac{2}{3}$ of 9 — 6

3. $\frac{2}{5}$ of 10 — 4

Write the mixed number or whole number for each improper fraction.

4. $\frac{13}{5}$ — $2\frac{3}{5}$

5. $\frac{15}{3}$ — 5

Write the improper fraction for each mixed number.

6. $3\frac{4}{5}$ — $\frac{19}{5}$

7. $2\frac{3}{4}$ — $\frac{11}{4}$

8. $2\frac{3}{5}$ — $\frac{13}{5}$

Write each fraction in simplest form.

9. $\frac{12}{15}$ — $\frac{4}{5}$

10. $\frac{10}{16}$ — $\frac{5}{8}$

11. Which fraction is in simplest form? — $\frac{2}{3}$
$\frac{3}{9}$ $\frac{4}{12}$ $\frac{2}{3}$ $\frac{8}{10}$

12. Which fraction is not in simplest form? — $\frac{5}{15}$
$\frac{5}{15}$ $\frac{5}{12}$ $\frac{5}{9}$ $\frac{5}{8}$

56

Name _____ Date _____

13. Multiply or divide to find the equivalent fraction.
$\frac{2}{4} = \frac{2 \times 4}{4 \times \boxed{4}} = \frac{\boxed{8}}{\boxed{16}}$

Compare. Write >, <, or = .

14. $\frac{9}{16}$ ⊙ $\frac{5}{16}$ >

15. $\frac{12}{5}$ ⊙ $\frac{24}{10}$ =

Add or subtract. Write the sum or difference in simplest form.

16. $\frac{3}{9} + \frac{4}{9} =$ — $\frac{7}{9}$

17. $\frac{2}{10} + \frac{6}{10} =$ — $\frac{4}{5}$

18. $2\frac{3}{5} + 3\frac{2}{5} =$ — 6

19. $4\frac{1}{6} + 3\frac{1}{6} =$ — $7\frac{1}{3}$

20. $\frac{7}{8} - \frac{3}{8} =$ — $\frac{1}{2}$

21. $\frac{4}{5} - \frac{1}{5} =$ — $\frac{3}{5}$

22. $8\frac{7}{9} - 7\frac{6}{9} =$ — $1\frac{1}{9}$

23. $2\frac{7}{8} - 1\frac{4}{8} =$ — $1\frac{3}{8}$

24. There are 18 players on Coach Allen's baseball team. Three players were injured in a game last week. What fraction of the players were not injured? Write the answer in simplest form.
— $\frac{5}{6}$

25. Suzie's grandmother made two pizzas. She cut each pizza into 8 pieces. After Suzie and three of her friends ate the pizzas, there was 1 piece of each left. Which mixed number describes the part of the two whole pizzas Suzie and her friends ate?
— $1\frac{7}{8}$

57

Name _____ Date _____

Fill in the ◯ for the correct answer.

1. Write the fraction for the shaded part. □ □ ▨ ▨ ▨
(A) $\frac{3}{5}$ (B) $\frac{2}{5}$ (C) $\frac{3}{10}$ (D) $\frac{2}{10}$

Find the fractional part of each number.

2. $\frac{2}{3}$ of 9 (F) 3 (G) 4 (H) 6 (J) 9

3. $\frac{2}{5}$ of 10 (A) 9 (B) 6 (C) 5 (D) 4

Write the mixed number or whole number for each improper fraction.

4. $\frac{13}{5}$ (F) $2\frac{3}{5}$ (G) $2\frac{3}{5}$ (H) $2\frac{1}{5}$ (J) $1\frac{3}{5}$

5. $\frac{15}{3}$ (A) $3\frac{3}{5}$ (B) $4\frac{1}{3}$ (C) $4\frac{2}{3}$ (D) 5

Write the improper fraction for each mixed number.

6. $3\frac{4}{5}$ (F) 19 (G) $\frac{23}{5}$ (H) $\frac{19}{5}$ (J) $\frac{17}{5}$

7. $2\frac{3}{4}$ (A) $\frac{10}{4}$ (B) $\frac{11}{4}$ (C) $\frac{14}{4}$ (D) 11

8. $2\frac{3}{5}$ (F) $\frac{10}{5}$ (G) $\frac{11}{5}$ (H) $\frac{13}{5}$ (J) 14

Write each fraction in simplest form.

9. $\frac{12}{15}$ (A) $\frac{5}{6}$ (B) $\frac{4}{5}$ (C) $\frac{2}{3}$ (D) $\frac{3}{5}$

10. $\frac{10}{16}$ (F) $\frac{5}{8}$ (G) $\frac{4}{10}$ (H) $\frac{2}{5}$ (J) $\frac{3}{8}$

58

Name _____ Date _____

11. Which fraction is in simplest form?
(A) $\frac{3}{9}$ (B) $\frac{4}{12}$ (C) $\frac{2}{3}$ (D) $\frac{8}{10}$

12. Which fraction is not in simplest form?
(F) $\frac{5}{15}$ (G) $\frac{5}{12}$ (H) $\frac{5}{9}$ (J) $\frac{5}{8}$

13. Multiply or divide to find the equivalent fraction.
$\frac{2}{4} = \frac{2 \times 4}{4 \times} =$ ▨▨
(A) 4, 8, 16 (B) 2, 4, 8 (C) 4, 8, 12 (D) 4, 4, 16

Which symbol makes each statement true?

14. $\frac{9}{16}$ ▨ $\frac{5}{16}$ (F) > (G) < (H) = (J) +

15. $\frac{12}{5}$ ▨ $\frac{24}{10}$ (A) > (B) < (C) = (D) +

Add or subtract. Write the sum or difference in simplest form.

16. $\frac{3}{9} + \frac{4}{9} =$ (F) 9 (G) $\frac{12}{9}$ (H) $\frac{7}{9}$ (J) $\frac{1}{9}$

17. $\frac{2}{10} + \frac{6}{10} =$ (A) $\frac{12}{10}$ (B) $\frac{8}{10}$ (C) $\frac{4}{5}$ (D) $\frac{4}{10}$

18. $2\frac{3}{5} + 3\frac{2}{5} =$ (F) 9 (G) $8\frac{3}{5}$ (H) $8\frac{2}{5}$ (J) $8\frac{1}{5}$

19. $4\frac{1}{6} + 3\frac{1}{6} =$ (A) $7\frac{2}{3}$ (B) $7\frac{4}{6}$ (C) $7\frac{4}{12}$ (D) $7\frac{1}{3}$

20. $\frac{7}{8} - \frac{3}{8} =$ (F) $1\frac{1}{4}$ (G) $\frac{10}{8}$ (H) $\frac{4}{8}$ (J) $\frac{1}{2}$

21. $\frac{4}{5} - \frac{1}{5} =$ (A) 1 (B) $\frac{3}{5}$ (C) $\frac{2}{5}$ (D) $\frac{1}{5}$

59

148

Chapter 7 Test, Form B

Name _____ Date _____

22. $8\frac{7}{9} - 7\frac{6}{9} =$ Ⓕ $12\frac{4}{9}$ Ⓖ $1\frac{1}{9}$
　　　　　　　　　Ⓗ $\frac{10}{9}$ Ⓙ $\frac{1}{9}$

23. $2\frac{7}{8} - 1\frac{4}{8} =$ Ⓐ $2\frac{3}{8}$ Ⓑ $1\frac{3}{8}$
　　　　　　　　　Ⓒ $1\frac{1}{8}$ Ⓓ $\frac{3}{8}$

24. There are 18 players on Coach Allen's baseball team. Three players were injured in a game last week. What fraction of the players were not injured? Write the answer in simplest form.
Ⓕ $\frac{3}{18}$ Ⓖ $\frac{3}{15}$
Ⓗ $\frac{5}{6}$ Ⓙ $5\frac{3}{18}$

25. Suzie's grandmother made two pizzas. She cut each pizza into 8 pieces. After Suzie and three of her friends ate the pizzas, there was 1 piece of each left. Which mixed number describes the part of the two whole pizzas Suzie and her friends ate?
Ⓐ $1\frac{7}{8}$ Ⓑ $1\frac{2}{3}$
Ⓒ $1\frac{1}{2}$ Ⓓ $1\frac{7}{8}$

60

Chapter 8 Pretest

Name _____ Date _____

Do you remember?

Write each fraction as a decimal.

1. $\frac{2}{10}$ _0.2_   **2.** $\frac{9}{10}$ _0.9_

3. $\frac{15}{100}$ _0.15_   **4.** $\frac{7}{100}$ _0.07_

Write a decimal for each shaded part.

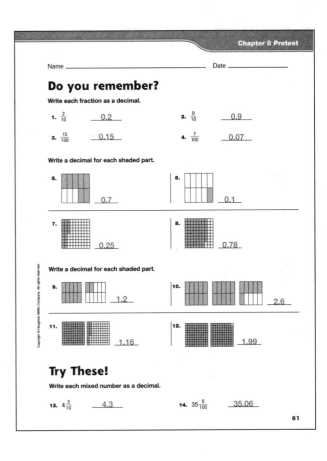

5. _0.7_   **6.** _0.1_

7. _0.25_   **8.** _0.78_

Write a decimal for each shaded part.

9. _1.2_   **10.** _2.6_

11. _1.16_   **12.** _1.99_

Try These!

Write each mixed number as a decimal.

13. $4\frac{3}{10}$ _4.3_   **14.** $35\frac{6}{100}$ _35.06_

61

Chapter 8 Pretest

Name _____ Date _____

Write a fraction and a decimal to describe each model.

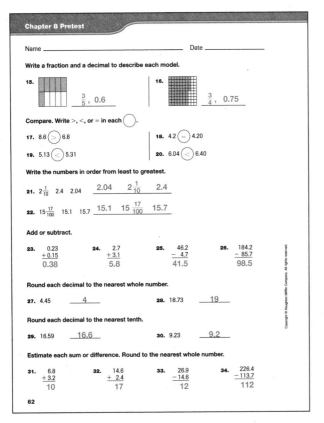

15. _$\frac{3}{5}$, 0.6_   **16.** _$\frac{3}{4}$, 0.75_

Compare. Write >, <, or = in each ◯.

17. 8.6 ⓥ> 6.8   **18.** 4.2 ⓥ= 4.20

19. 5.13 ⓥ< 5.31   **20.** 6.04 ⓥ< 6.40

Write the numbers in order from least to greatest.

21. $2\frac{1}{10}$ 2.4 2.04   _2.04 $2\frac{1}{10}$ 2.4_

22. $15\frac{17}{100}$ 15.1 15.7   _15.1 $15\frac{17}{100}$ 15.7_

Add or subtract.

23. $\begin{array}{r} 0.23 \\ + 0.15 \\ \hline 0.38 \end{array}$ **24.** $\begin{array}{r} 2.7 \\ + 3.1 \\ \hline 5.8 \end{array}$ **25.** $\begin{array}{r} 46.2 \\ - 4.7 \\ \hline 41.5 \end{array}$ **26.** $\begin{array}{r} 184.2 \\ - 85.7 \\ \hline 98.5 \end{array}$

Round each decimal to the nearest whole number.

27. 4.45   _4_   **28.** 18.73   _19_

Round each decimal to the nearest tenth.

29. 16.59   _16.6_   **30.** 9.23   _9.2_

Estimate each sum or difference. Round to the nearest whole number.

31. $\begin{array}{r} 6.8 \\ + 3.2 \\ \hline 10 \end{array}$ **32.** $\begin{array}{r} 14.6 \\ + 2.4 \\ \hline 17 \end{array}$ **33.** $\begin{array}{r} 26.9 \\ - 14.6 \\ \hline 12 \end{array}$ **34.** $\begin{array}{r} 226.4 \\ - 113.7 \\ \hline 112 \end{array}$

62

Chapter 8 Test, Form A

Name _____ Date _____

Write the correct answer.

Write each mixed number as a decimal.

1. $4\frac{30}{100}$ _4.30_   **2.** $2\frac{6}{10}$ _2.6_   **3.** $31\frac{50}{100}$ _31.50_

4. Write the correct decimal for the following amount.
one and forty-two hundredths   _1.42_

Write a mixed number for the following amount.

5. one and forty-two hundredths   _$1\frac{42}{100}$_

Compare. Write >, <, or =.

6. 4.1 ⓥ< 4.11   **7.** 7.50 ⓥ= 7.5

8. 0.2 ⓥ> $\frac{2}{100}$ **9.** 3.26 ⓥ= $3\frac{26}{100}$

10. Order from least to greatest.
1   $2\frac{1}{2}$ 2.25   2
1   2   2.25 $2\frac{1}{2}$

11. Order from greatest to least.
$12\frac{2}{100}$ 12.04   12.4 $12\frac{2}{10}$
12.4 $12\frac{2}{10}$ 12.04 $12\frac{2}{100}$

63

149

Name _____ Date _____

Add or subtract.

12.	**13.**	**14.**	**15.**	**16.**
5.6 + 2.8 **8.4**	12.23 + 8.82 **21.05**	135.06 + 237.95 **373.01**	17.7 − 9.2 **8.5**	26.04 − 19.22 **6.82**

17. Round 25.7 to the nearest whole number. __26__

18. Round 16.85 to the nearest tenth. __16.9__

Estimate each sum or difference. Round to the nearest whole number.

19.	**20.**	**21.**	**22.**
6.8 + 7.2 **14**	172.7 + 135.2 **308**	24.2 − 18.8 **5**	245.1 − 121.7 **123**

23. Janie earns $4.00 babysitting. She saves $2.15 of her earnings and spends the rest. How much does she spend?

__$1.85__

24. Jim is buying a package of sliced turkey for $3.49. If Jim has $10, how much money will he have left after buying the turkey?

__$6.51__

25. Beth's basketball team is raising money. The first week, Beth and her teammates raised $10. The second week, they raised $20. The third week, they raised $30. If the pattern continued, during which week will they raise $80?

__eighth__

Name _____ Date _____

Fill in the ◯ for the correct answer.

Choose the correct decimal for each mixed number.

1. $4\frac{30}{100}$

(A) 4.03   (B) 4.30   (C) 43.0   (D) 430.0

2. $2\frac{6}{10}$

(F) 261.0   (G) 26.0   (H) 2.6   (J) 0.26

3. $31\frac{50}{100}$

(A) 3.15   (B) 31.50   (C) 315.0   (D) 31,500.0

4. Choose the correct decimal for the following amount. one and forty-two hundredths

(F) 142.0   (G) 4.2
(H) 1.42   (J) 0.142

5. Choose the correct mixed number for the following amount. one and forty-two hundredths

(A) $\frac{142}{1,000}$ (B) $14\frac{2}{10}$
(C) $\frac{142}{100}$ (D) $1\frac{42}{100}$

Which symbol makes each statement true?

6. 4.1 ⬤ 4.11

(F) >   (G) <   (H) =   (J) +

7. 7.50 ⬤ 7.5

(A) >   (B) <   (C) =   (D) +

Name _____ Date _____

8. 0.2 ◯ $\frac{2}{100}$

(F) >   (G) <   (H) =   (J) +

9. 3.26 ◯ $3\frac{26}{100}$

(A) >   (B) <   (C) =   (D) +

10. Order from least to greatest.

1    $2\frac{1}{2}$ 2.25   2

(F) 1   2 $2\frac{1}{2}$ 2.25
(G) 1   2   2.25 $2\frac{1}{2}$
(H) 2.25 $2\frac{1}{2}$ 2   1
(J) $2\frac{1}{2}$ 2.25   2   1

11. Order from greatest to least.

$12\frac{2}{100}$ 12.04   12.4 $12\frac{2}{10}$

(A) 12.04   12.4 $12\frac{2}{100}$ $12\frac{2}{10}$
(B) 12.04 $12\frac{2}{100}$ 12.4 $12\frac{2}{10}$
(C) 12.4 $12\frac{2}{100}$ 12.04 $12\frac{2}{10}$
(D) 12.4 $12\frac{2}{10}$ 12.04 $12\frac{2}{100}$

Name _____ Date _____

Add or subtract.

12. 5.6
 + 2.8

(F) 8.4   (G) 8.2   (H) 7.4   (J) 7.2

13. 12.23
 + 8.82

(A) 20.05   (B) 20.5   (C) 21.05   (D) 21.5

14. 135.06
 + 237.95

(F) 362.01   (G) 362.91   (H) 372.01   (J) 373.01

15. 17.7
 − 9.2

(A) 12.5   (B) 8.5   (C) 7.5   (D) 2.5

16. 26.04
 − 19.22

(F) 16.82   (G) 13.82   (H) 6.82   (J) 3.72

17. Round 25.7 to the nearest whole number.

(A) 2,570   (B) 257   (C) 26   (D) 25

18. Round 16.85 to the nearest tenth.

(F) 16.9   (G) 168.5   (H) 169.0   (J) 1,685.0

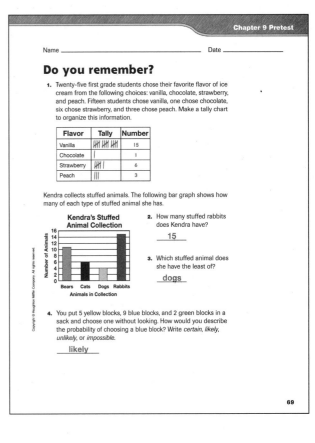

Name _____ Date _____

Estimate each sum or difference. Round to the nearest whole number.

19.   6.8
        + 7.2

(A) 12   (B) 13   (C) 14 ✓   (D) 15

20.   172.7
        + 135.2

(F) 37.5   (G) 307.9   (H) 308 ✓   (J) 400

21.   24.2
        − 18.8

(A) 5 ✓   (B) 6   (C) 44   (D) 45

22.   245.1
        − 121.7

(F) 366.8   (G) 123.4   (H) 124   (J) 123 ✓

23. Janie earns $4.00 babysitting. She saves $\frac{3}{5}$ of her earnings and spends the rest. How much does she spend?

(A) $5.60   (B) $3.65   (C) $0.35   (D) $1.60 ✓

24. Jim is buying a package of sliced turkey for $3.49. If Jim has $10, how much money will he have left after buying the turkey?

(F) $7.51   (G) $6.51 ✓   (H) $4.39   (J) $3.39

25. Beth's basketball team is raising money. The first week, Beth and her team-mates raised $10. The second week, they raised $20. The third week, they raised $30. If the pattern continued, during which week will they raise $80?

(A) fifth   (B) sixth   (C) seventh   (D) eighth ✓

68

Name _____ Date _____

Do you remember?

1. Twenty-five first grade students chose their favorite flavor of ice cream from the following choices: vanilla, chocolate, strawberry, and peach. Fifteen students chose vanilla, one chose chocolate, six chose strawberry, and three chose peach. Make a tally chart to organize this information.

Flavor	Tally	Number
Vanilla	IIII IIII IIII	15
Chocolate	I	1
Strawberry	IIII I	6
Peach	III	3

Kendra collects stuffed animals. The following bar graph shows how many of each type of stuffed animal she has.

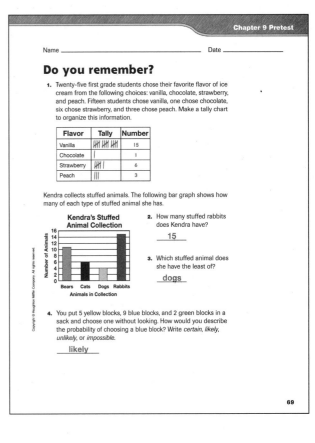

2. How many stuffed rabbits does Kendra have?

_____15_____

3. Which stuffed animal does she have the least of?

_____dogs_____

4. You put 5 yellow blocks, 9 blue blocks, and 2 green blocks in a sack and choose one without looking. How would you describe the probability of choosing a blue block? Write *certain*, *likely*, *unlikely*, or *impossible*.

_____likely_____

69

Name _____ Date _____

Try These!

Find the range, mode, median, and mean.

5. 3, 5, 3, 9

_____range = 6, mode = 3, median = 4, mean = 5_____

6. 10, 15, 5, 15, 20

_____range = 15, mode = 15, median = 15, mean = 13_____

Use the graph below for Questions 7 and 8.

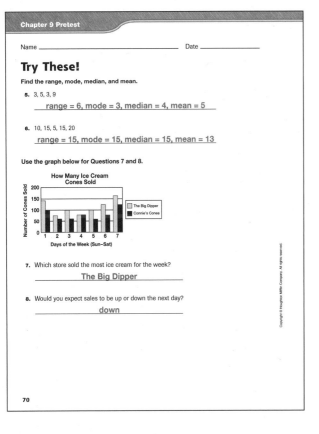

7. Which store sold the most ice cream for the week?

_____The Big Dipper_____

8. Would you expect sales to be up or down the next day?

_____down_____

70

Name _____ Date _____

Use the graph below for Questions 9 and 10.

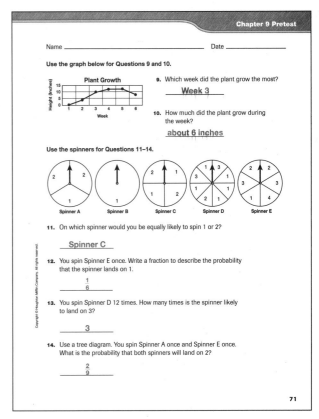

9. Which week did the plant grow the most?

_____Week 3_____

10. How much did the plant grow during the week?

_____about 6 inches_____

Use the spinners for Questions 11–14.

11. On which spinner would you be equally likely to spin 1 or 2?

_____Spinner C_____

12. You spin Spinner E once. Write a fraction to describe the probability that the spinner lands on 1.

_____$\frac{1}{6}$_____

13. You spin Spinner D 12 times. How many times is the spinner likely to land on 3?

_____3_____

14. Use a tree diagram. You spin Spinner A once and Spinner E once. What is the probability that both spinners will land on 2?

_____$\frac{2}{9}$_____

71

Answer Key

Name _____ Date _____

Write the correct answer.

Find the range, mode, median, and mean. Then identify any outliers.

1. 4, 10, 6, 4 _range = 6; mode = 4; median = 5; mean = 6; no outliers_

2. 40, 50, 45, 90, 45
   range = 50; mode = 45; median = 45; mean = 54; outlier = 90

Use the graph for Questions 3–6.

3. In which month was the difference between the number of books read by fourth graders and fifth graders the greatest?

   April

4. In which month did the fourth and fifth graders read the same number of books?

   March

5. Who read more books in all, the fourth graders or fifth graders? How many more did they read?

   fourth; 100

6. There are 50 fourth graders. What is the mean of the of books read by fourth graders in January?

   _3_

Reading Contest

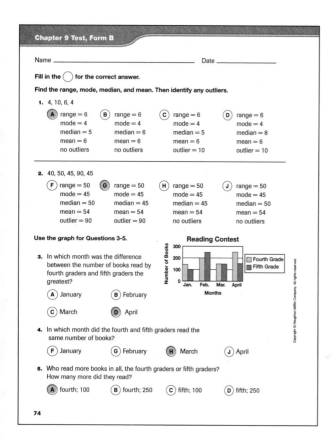

Use the graph for Questions 7–10.

7. Between which two times did the temperature change the most?

   8 AM and 10 AM

8. At what time was the temperature 45°F?

   _10 AM_

9. Between which two times did the temperature stay the same?

   _12 PM to 2 PM_

10. How many degrees did the temperature decrease from 2 PM to 4 PM?

    _10_

72

Name _____ Date _____

A bag contains 1 green marble, 3 red marbles, and 4 yellow marbles. Write certain, likely, unlikely, or impossible for Questions 11–13.

11. What is the probability of choosing a green marble from the bag? _unlikely_

12. What is the probability of choosing a blue marble from the bag? _impossible_

13. What is the probability of choosing a yellow marble from the bag? _likely_

Use the spinner below for Questions 14–16. Write the correct answer.

14. What is the probability of spinning a "3"? $\frac{1}{8}$

15. What is the probability of spinning a "2"? $\frac{5}{8}$

16. What is the probability of spinning a "1"? $\frac{1}{4}$

You write each of the letters P, R, O, B, A, B, I, L, I, T, Y on a card and place the cards in a bag.

17. If you pick a card without looking, which two letters are you most likely to pick? _B and I_

18. If you pick a card and put it back 44 times, how many times would you probably pick the letter "T"? _4_

19. Bryan and Kyle live on Oak Street. Kyle lives 8 blocks from Lion's Park and Bryan lives 3 blocks on the other side of Lion's Park. If Kyle rides his bike to Bryan's house and back home, how many blocks does he ride on the round trip? _22_

20. You spin Spinner A and then spin Spinner B. If you do this 32 times, how many times will you probably spin a 3 on both spinners?

    _2_

Spinner A   Spinner B

73

Name _____ Date _____

Fill in the ◯ for the correct answer.

Find the range, mode, median, and mean. Then identify any outliers.

1. 4, 10, 6, 4

   (A) range = 6
   mode = 4
   median = 5
   mean = 6
   no outliers

   (B) range = 6
   mode = 4
   median = 6
   mean = 6
   no outliers

   (C) range = 6
   mode = 4
   median = 5
   mean = 6
   outlier = 10

   (D) range = 6
   mode = 4
   median = 8
   mean = 6
   outlier = 10

2. 40, 50, 45, 90, 45

   (F) range = 50
   mode = 45
   median = 50
   mean = 54
   outlier = 90

   (G) range = 50
   mode = 45
   median = 45
   mean = 54
   outlier = 90

   (H) range = 50
   mode = 45
   median = 45
   mean = 54
   no outliers

   (J) range = 50
   mode = 45
   median = 50
   mean = 54
   no outliers

Use the graph for Questions 3–5.

Reading Contest

3. In which month was the difference between the number of books read by fourth graders and fifth graders the greatest?

   (A) January   (B) February
   (C) March   (D) April

4. In which month did the fourth and fifth graders read the same number of books?

   (F) January   (G) February   (H) March   (J) April

5. Who read more books in all, the fourth graders or fifth graders? How many more did they read?

   (A) fourth; 100   (B) fourth; 250   (C) fifth; 100   (D) fifth; 250

74

Name _____ Date _____

6. There are 50 fourth graders. What is the mean of the number of books read by fourth graders in January?

   (A) 150   (B) 50   (C) 15   (D) 3

Use the graph for Questions 7–10.

7. Between which two times did the temperature change the most?

   (F) 8 AM to 10 AM   (G) 10 AM to 12 PM
   (H) 12 PM to 2 PM   (J) 2 PM to 4 PM

Temperature on Monday

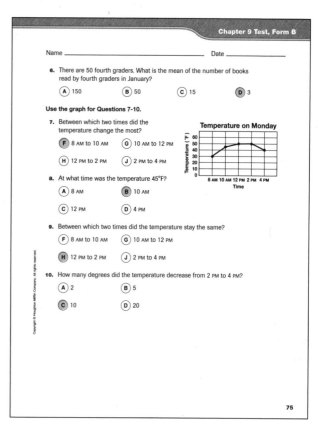

8. At what time was the temperature 45°F?

   (A) 8 AM   (B) 10 AM
   (C) 12 PM   (D) 4 PM

9. Between which two times did the temperature stay the same?

   (F) 8 AM to 10 AM   (G) 10 AM to 12 PM
   (H) 12 PM to 2 PM   (J) 2 PM to 4 PM

10. How many degrees did the temperature decrease from 2 PM to 4 PM?

    (A) 2   (B) 5
    (C) 10   (D) 20

75

152

Chapter 9 Test, Form B

Name _____ Date _____

A bag contains 1 green marble, 3 red marbles, and 4 yellow marbles. Choose *certain*, *likely*, *unlikely*, or *impossible* for Questions 11-13.

11. What is the probability of choosing a green marble from the bag?
   (A) certain (B) likely
   (C) unlikely (D) impossible

12. What is the probability of choosing a blue marble from the bag?
   (F) certain (G) likely
   (H) unlikely **(J) impossible**

13. What is the probability of choosing a yellow marble from the bag?
   (A) certain **(B) likely**
   (C) unlikely (D) impossible

Use the spinner below for Questions 14-16.

14. What is the probability of spinning a "3"?
   (F) $\frac{1}{8}$ (G) $\frac{3}{12}$ (H) $\frac{3}{8}$ (J) $\frac{3}{7}$

15. What is the probability of spinning a "2"?
   (A) $\frac{1}{8}$ (B) $\frac{3}{8}$ (C) $\frac{6}{8}$ **(D)** $\frac{5}{8}$

16. What is the probability of spinning a "1"?
   (F) $\frac{1}{8}$ **(G)** $\frac{1}{4}$ (H) $\frac{1}{2}$ (J) $\frac{6}{8}$

76

Chapter 9 Test, Form B

Name _____ Date _____

You write each of the letters P, R, O, B, A, B, I, L, I, T, and Y on a card and place the cards in a bag.

17. If you pick a card without looking, which two letters are you most likely to pick?
   (A) P and Y (B) L and O **(C) B and I** (D) A and R

18. If you pick a card and put it back 44 times, how many times would you probably pick the letter "T"?
   (F) 22 (G) 11 (H) 10 **(J) 4**

19. Bryan and Kyle live on Oak Street. Kyle lives 8 blocks from Lion's Park and Bryan lives 3 blocks on the other side of Lion's Park. If Kyle rides his bike to Bryan's house and back home, how many blocks does he ride on the round trip?
   (A) 5 (B) 11 **(C) 22** (D) 24

20. Spin Spinner A and then spin Spinner B. If you do this 32 times, how many times will you probably spin a 3 on both spinners?
   (F) 2 (G) 4 (H) 6 (J) 8

77

Chapter 10 Pretest

Name _____ Date _____

Do you remember?

Name each figure.

1. ___triangle___
2. ___rectangle___

Name each solid figure.

3. ___rectangular prism___
4. ___cone___

Draw the other half of each figure.

5. 6.

Try These!

Write *parallel*, *intersecting*, or *perpendicular* to describe the relationship between each pair of lines.

7. ___perpendicular___
8. ___parallel___

Write *acute*, *right*, or *obtuse* to describe each angle.

9. ___acute___
10. ___right___

78

Chapter 10 Pretest

Name _____ Date _____

11. Name the quadrilateral with the most specific name possible.
   ___rhombus___

12. Name the triangle by both its angles and its sides.
   ___obtuse, scalene___

13. Name the part of the circle shown by the segment in the figure below.
   ___radius___

14. Are the two figures congruent? Write yes or no.
   ___yes___

Write *line symmetry*, *rotational symmetry*, or *no symmetry* to describe each figure.

15. ___rotational symmetry___
16. ___line symmetry___

Use the figure below for Questions 17 and 18.

17. Find the perimeter. ___18 ft___
18. Find the area. ___14 ft²___

19. Name the solid figure that can be made with the following net.
   ___cube___

Use the figure below for Questions 20 and 21.

20. Find the surface area. ___40 in.²___
21. Find the volume. ___16 in.³___

79

153

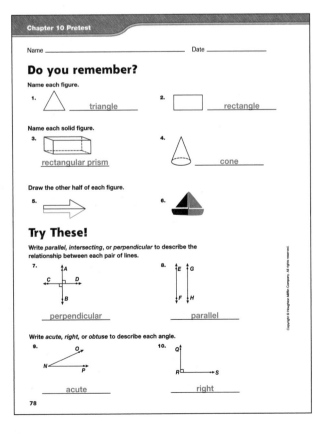
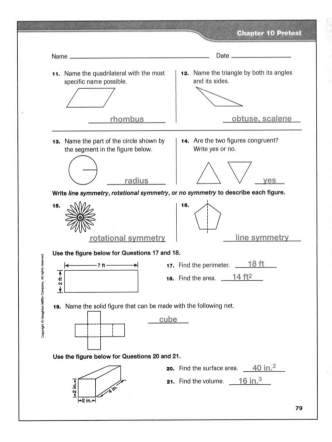

Answer Key

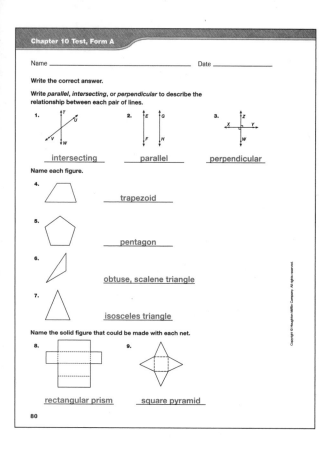

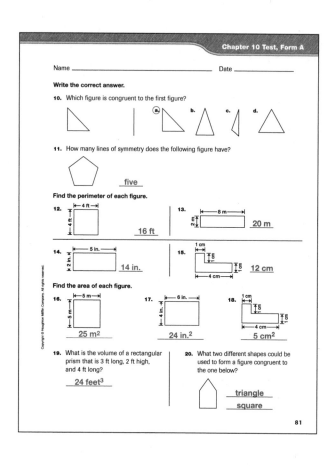

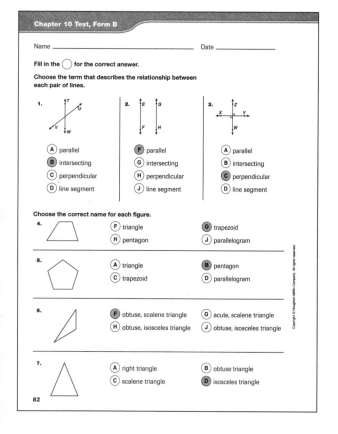

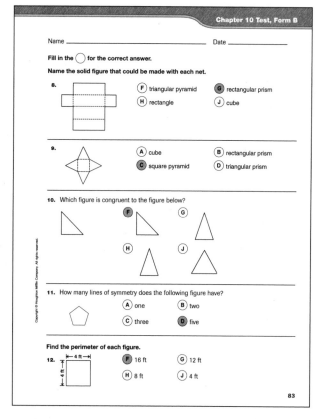

Chapter 10 Test, Form B

Name _____ Date _____

Fill in the ◯ for the correct answer.

13. |← 8 m →| 2 m
   (A) 10 m (B) 16 m
   (C) 20 m (D) 24 m

14. |← 5 in. →| 2 in.
   (F) 14 in. (G) 10 in.
   (H) 7 in. (J) 3 in.

15. 1 cm ... 4 cm
   (A) 10 cm (B) 11 cm
   (C) 12 cm (D) 13 cm

Find the area of each figure.

16. 5 m square
   (F) 25 m² (G) 25 m²
   (H) 15 m² (J) 10 m²

17. 6 in. × 4 in.
   (A) 10 in.² (B) 20 in.²
   (C) 24 in.² (D) 36 in.²

18. 1 cm ... 4 cm
   (F) 8 cm² (G) 5 cm²
   (H) 4 cm² (J) 2 cm²

19. What is the volume of a rectangular prism that is 3 ft long, 2 ft high, and 4 ft wide?
   (A) 6 ft³ (B) 9 ft³ (C) 10 ft³ (D) 24 ft³

20. What two different shapes could be used to form a figure congruent to the one below?
   (F) square and rectangle (G) square and triangle
   (H) square and trapezoid (J) pentagon and rectangle

84

Chapter 11 Pretest

Name _____ Date _____

Do you remember?

Use the graph below for Questions 1–4.

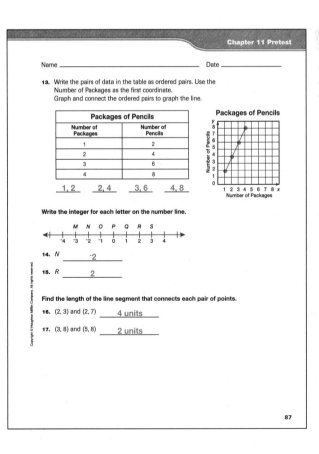

1. You are at the school. Should you go up, down, right, or left to get to the fire station?
   __up__

2. You are at the police station. Should you go up, down, right, or left to get to the school?
   __left__

3. You are at the fire station. Should you go up, down, right, or left to get to the swimming pool?
   __right__

4. You are at the swimming pool. Should you go up, down, right, or left to get to the police station?
   __down__

85

Chapter 11 Pretest

Name _____ Date _____

Use the number line for Questions 5 and 6.

A B C D E F G H I
0 1 2 3 4 5 6 7 8 9 10

5. Write the integer for the letter C. __3__

6. Write the letter at 6. __F__

Use the rule to complete each table.

7. | n | n + 2 |
   |---|---|
   | 1 | 3 |
   | 2 | 4 |
   | 3 | 5 |
   | 4 | 6 |

8. | n | 3n |
   |---|---|
   | 1 | 3 |
   | 2 | 6 |
   | 3 | 9 |
   | 4 | 12 |

Try These!

Write the letter of the point for each ordered pair.

9. (3, 5) __B__

10. (2, 1) __A__

Plot each point and label it with the correct letter.

11. F (3, 1)

12. K (7, 5)

86

Chapter 11 Pretest

Name _____ Date _____

13. Write the pairs of data in the table as ordered pairs. Use the Number of Packages as the first coordinate.
   Graph and connect the ordered pairs to graph the line.

Packages of Pencils

Number of Packages	Number of Pencils
1	2
2	4
3	6
4	8

__1, 2__ __2, 4__ __3, 6__ __4, 8__

Write the integer for each letter on the number line.

M N O P Q R S
-4 -3 -2 -1 0 1 2 3 4

14. N __-2__

15. R __2__

Find the length of the line segment that connects each pair of points.

16. (2, 3) and (2, 7) __4 units__

17. (3, 8) and (5, 8) __2 units__

87

Answer Key

Name _____ Date _____

Write the correct answer.

Use the graph for Questions 1–5.

1. Write the letter of the point named by the ordered pair (6, 7). ____*B*____

2. Write the letter of the point named by the ordered pair (9, 4). ____*C*____

3. What are the coordinates of point *A* ? ___(3, 1)___

4. What are the coordinates of point *D* ? ___(9, 10)___

5. What are the coordinates of point *E* ? ___(1, 3)___

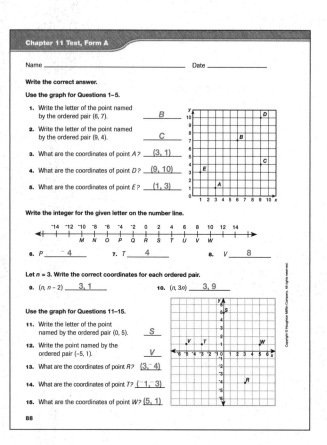

Write the integer for the given letter on the number line.

6. *P* ___−4___   7. *T* ___4___   8. *V* ___8___

Let *n* = 3. Write the correct coordinates for each ordered pair.

9. (*n*, *n* − 2) ___3, 1___   10. (*n*, 3*n*) ___3, 9___

Use the graph for Questions 11–15.

11. Write the letter of the point named by the ordered pair (0, 5). ___*S*___

12. Write the point named by the ordered pair (−5, 1). ___*V*___

13. What are the coordinates of point *R*? ___(3, −4)___

14. What are the coordinates of point *T*? ___(−1, −3)___

15. What are the coordinates of point *W*? ___(5, 1)___

88

Name _____ Date _____

Find the length of the line segment that connects each pair of points.

16. (4, 2) and (4, 10) ___8 units___

17. (−1, 1) and (−1, 7) ___6 units___

18. (5, 8) and (8, 8) ___3 units___

19. Write an ordered pair that describes a point on the line graphed at right.
___possible answer: (1, 2)___

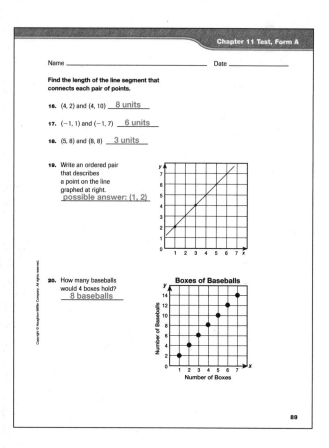

20. How many baseballs would 4 boxes hold?
___8 baseballs___

Boxes of Baseballs

89

Name _____ Date _____

Fill in the ◯ for the correct answer.

Use the graph for Questions 1–5.

1. Choose the letter of the point named by the ordered pair (6, 7).
Ⓐ *B* Ⓑ *C* Ⓒ *D* Ⓓ *E*

2. Choose the letter of the point named by the ordered pair (9, 4).
Ⓕ *A* Ⓖ *B* Ⓗ *C* Ⓙ *D*

3. What are the coordinates of point *A*?
Ⓐ (3, 1) Ⓑ (1, 3) Ⓒ (0, 3) Ⓓ (3, 0)

4. What are the coordinates of point *D*?
Ⓕ (9, 8) Ⓖ (8, 9) Ⓗ (10, 9) Ⓙ (9, 10)

5. What are the coordinates of point *E*?
Ⓐ (3, 1) Ⓑ (1, 3) Ⓒ (0, 3) Ⓓ (3, 0)

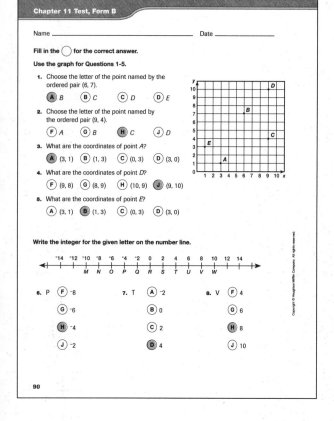

Write the integer for the given letter on the number line.

6. P Ⓕ −8   7. T Ⓐ −2   8. V Ⓕ 4
   Ⓖ −6   Ⓑ 0   Ⓖ 6
   Ⓗ −4   Ⓒ 2   Ⓗ 8
   Ⓙ −2   Ⓓ 4   Ⓙ 10

90

Name _____ Date _____

Let *n* = 3. Choose the correct coordinates for each ordered pair.

9. (*n*, *n* −2)
Ⓐ (3, −6) Ⓑ (3, 1) Ⓒ (3, 5) Ⓓ (3, 6)

10. (*n*, 3*n*)
Ⓕ (3, 9) Ⓖ (3, 6) Ⓗ (3, 0) Ⓙ (3, −6)

Use the graph below for Questions 11–15.

11. Choose the letter of the point named by the ordered pair (0, 10).
Ⓐ *R* Ⓑ *S*
Ⓒ *T* Ⓓ *V*

12. Choose the letter of the point named by the ordered pair (−5, 1).
Ⓕ *S* Ⓖ *T*
Ⓗ *V* Ⓙ *W*

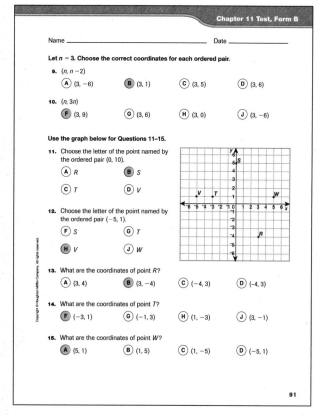

13. What are the coordinates of point *R*?
Ⓐ (3, 4) Ⓑ (3, −4) Ⓒ (−4, 3) Ⓓ (-4, 3)

14. What are the coordinates of point *T*?
Ⓕ (−3, 1) Ⓖ (−1, 3) Ⓗ (1, −3) Ⓙ (3, −1)

15. What are the coordinates of point *W*?
Ⓐ (5, 1) Ⓑ (1, 5) Ⓒ (1, −5) Ⓓ (−5, 1)

91

156

Chapter 11 Test, Form B

Name _____ Date _____

Find the length of the line segment that connects each pair of points.

16. (4, 2) and (4, 10)

Ⓕ 8   Ⓖ 12   Ⓗ 16   Ⓙ 20

17. (−1, 1) and (−1, 7)

Ⓐ 2   Ⓑ 6   Ⓒ 8   Ⓓ 9

18. (5, 8) and (8, 8)

Ⓕ 0   Ⓖ 3   Ⓗ 13   Ⓙ 16

19. Which ordered pair describes a point on the line graphed on the right?

Ⓐ (1, 2)   Ⓑ (1, 3)

Ⓒ (2, 1)   Ⓓ (3, 1)

Use the graph to solve the problem.

20. How many baseballs would 4 boxes hold?

Ⓕ 4   Ⓖ 6   Ⓗ 8   Ⓙ 10

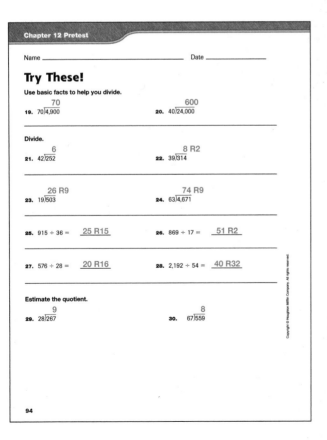

92

Chapter 12 Pretest

Name _____ Date _____

Write the correct answer.

Do you remember?

Add, subtract, multiply, or divide.

1. 9 + 4 = ___13___   **2.** 4 + 8 = ___12___

3. 4 + 7 = ___11___   **4.** 9 + 6 = ___15___

5. 15 − 8 = ___7___   **6.** 12 − 7 = ___5___

7. 13 − 5 = ___8___   **8.** 16 − 7 = ___9___

9. 6 × 7 = ___42___   **10.** 7 × 4 = ___28___

11. 8 × 8 = ___64___   **12.** 3 × 8 = ___24___

13. 32 ÷ 4 = ___8___   **14.** 63 ÷ 7 = ___9___

15. 49 ÷ 7 = ___7___   **16.** 24 ÷ 6 = ___4___

17. 6)64 10R4   **18.** 9)297 33

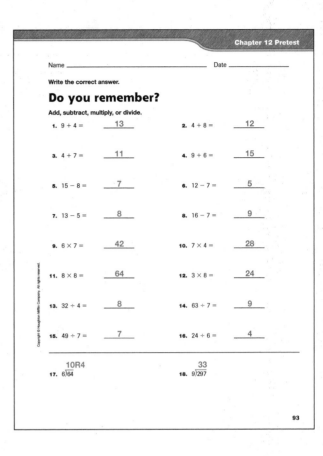

93

Chapter 12 Pretest

Name _____ Date _____

Try These!

Use basic facts to help you divide.

19. 70)4,900 70   **20.** 40)24,000 600

Divide.

21. 42)252 6   **22.** 39)314 8 R2

23. 19)503 26 R9   **24.** 63)4,671 74 R9

25. 915 ÷ 36 = ___25 R15___   **26.** 869 ÷ 17 = ___51 R2___

27. 576 ÷ 28 = ___20 R16___   **28.** 2,192 ÷ 54 = ___40 R32___

Estimate the quotient.

29. 28)267 9   **30.** 67)559 8

94

Chapter 12 Test, Form A

Name _____ Date _____

Write the correct answer.

Use basic facts to help you divide.

1. 70)56,000 800   **2.** 6)2,400 400

Divide.

3. 18)72 4   **4.** 78)702 9

5. 39)195 5   **6.** 27)93 3 R12

7. 59)248 4 R12   **8.** 52)425 8 R9

Compare. Write >, <, or =.

9. 728 ÷ 28 ⊃ 728 ÷ 82   **10.** 360 ÷ 40 ⊜ 540 ÷ 60

Divide.

11. 23)742 32 R6   **12.** 46)992 21 R26

13. 38)2,136 56 R8   **14.** 92)6,729 73 R13

15. 39)774 19 R33   **16.** 43)819 19 R2

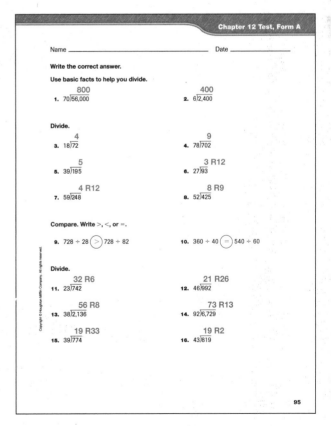

95

Answer Key

Name _____ Date _____

Write the correct answer.

17. 2,014 ÷ 68 = __29 R42__   **18.** 8,113 ÷ 92 = __88 R17__

19. 703 ÷ 64 = __10 R 63__   **20.** 792 ÷ 38 = __20 R32__

21. 5,209 ÷ 74 = __70 R29__   **22.** 4,703 ÷ 52 = __90 R23__

23. There are 118 fourth grade students and 143 fifth grade students who eat lunch at the same time. If 12 students can sit at one lunch table, how many tables are needed to seat all of the students?

_____22 tables_____

24. A bakery bakes 875 loaves of bread each day. Each loaf is sliced and is cut 19 times. How many slices of bread do they have in all ?

_____17,500 slices_____

25. The cafeteria serves 1,840 cartons of milk each week. If the same number of cartons are served each day, how many cartons are served in one day?

_____368 cartons_____

96

Name _____ Date _____

Fill in the ◯ for the correct answer.

Use basic facts to help you divide.

1. 70)56,000 — (A) 8,000   (B) 800 ●   (C) 80   (D) 8

2. 6)2,400 — (F) 4,000   (G) 400 ●   (H) 40   (J) 4

Divide.

3. 18)72 — (A) 2   (B) 3   (C) 4 ●   (D) 6

4. 78)702 — (F) 6   (G) 7   (H) 8   (J) 9 ●

5. 39)195 — (A) 5 ●   (B) 4   (C) 3   (D) 2

6. 27)93 — (F) 30 R 12   (G) 4 R 5   (H) 3 R 12 ●   (J) 3 R 3

7. 59)248 — (A) 4 R 8   (B) 4 R 12 ●   (C) 5 R 53   (D) 40 R 12

8. 52)425 — (F) 8 R 9 ●   (G) 8 R 25   (H) 80 R 9   (J) 80 R 25

Which symbol makes each statement true?

9. 728 ÷ 28 ● 728 ÷ 82   (A) > ●   (B) <   (C) =   (D) +

10. 360 ÷ 40 ● 540 ÷ 60   (F) >   (G) <   (H) = ●   (J) +

Divide.

11. 23)742 — (A) 320 R 6   (B) 36 R 14   (C) 32 R 14   (D) 32 R 6 ●

12. 46)992 — (F) 19 R 18   (G) 20 R 2   (H) 21 R 26 ●   (J) 22 R 20

13. 38)2,136 — (A) 49 R 34   (B) 56 R 8 ●   (C) 56 R 12   (D) 506 R 8

14. 92)6,729 — (F) 73 R 13 ●   (G) 73 R 53   (H) 704 R 61   (J) 730 R 13

15. 39)774 — (A) 13 R 3   (B) 19 R 33 ●   (C) 20 R 14   (D) 22 R 26

16. 43)819 — (F) 23 R 30   (G) 21 R 16   (H) 19 R 42   (J) 19 R 2 ●

97

Name _____ Date _____

Divide.

17. 2,014 ÷ 68 = ▩   (A) 25 R 14   (B) 29 R 42 ●   (C) 30 R 34   (D) 32 R 48

18. 8,113 ÷ 92 = ▩   (F) 88 R 17 ●   (G) 88 R 27   (H) 89 R 25   (J) 90 R 73

19. 703 ÷ 64 = ▩   (A) 12 R 45   (B) 12 R 25   (C) 11 R 1   (D) 10 R 63 ●

20. 792 ÷ 38 = ▩   (F) 2 R 32   (G) 20 R 13   (H) 20 R 32 ●   (J) 21 R 6

21. 5,209 ÷ 74 = ▩   (A) 72 R 41   (B) 71 R 55   (C) 70 R 29 ●   (D) 7 R 29

22. 4,703 ÷ 52 = ▩   (F) 90 R 23 ●   (G) 91 R 31   (H) 94 R 15   (J) 95 R 33

Solve.

23. There are 118 fourth grade students and 143 fifth grade students who eat lunch at the same time. If 12 students can sit at one lunch table, how many tables are needed to seat all of the students?

(A) 37 tables   (B) 25 tables   (C) 22 tables ●   (D) 20 tables

24. A bakery bakes 875 loaves of bread each day. Each loaf is sliced and is cut 19 times. How many slices of bread do they have in all ?

(F) 17,500 slices ●   (G) 16,625 slices   (H) 894 slices   (J) 856 slices

25. The cafeteria serves 1,840 cartons of milk each week. If the same number of cartons are served each day, how many cartons are served in one day?

(A) 206 cartons   (B) 260 cartons   (C) 316 cartons   (D) 368 cartons ●

98

Name _____ Date _____

Choose the correct answer.

1. What is the word form of 62,008,429?

(A) sixty-two million, 8 thousand, four hundred twenty nine ●

(B) sixty-two billion, 8 million, four hundred twenty nine

(C) six billion, two million, eight thousand, four hundred twenty nine

(D) six hundred two million, eight thousand, four hundred twenty nine

Which symbol makes each statement true?

2. 588,700 ● 587,800   (F) > ●   (G) <   (H) =   (J) +

3. 3,040,600 ● 3,100,600   (A) >   (B) < ●   (C) =   (D) +

4. Which numbers are ordered from least to greatest?

(F) 74,085   72,085   72,580   (G) 72,580   72,085   74,085

(H) 72,085   74,085   72,580   (J) 72,085   72,580   74,085 ●

5. Round 254,718 to the nearest ten thousand.

(A) 240,000   (B) 250,000 ●   (C) 254,000   (D) 255,000

6. Thomasine bought fruit for $5.12. She paid with a $10 bill. What change should she have received?

(F) 3 pennies, 1 dime, 1 quarter, 1 half-dollar, 5 one dollar bills

(G) 3 pennies, 1 dime, 2 quarters, 4 one dollar bills

(H) 3 pennies, 1 dime, 1 quarter, 1 half-dollar, 4 one dollar bills ●

(J) 3 pennies, 3 dimes, 1 half-dollar, 4 one dollar bills

99

158

Quarterly Test 1

Name _____ Date _____

7. Anna, Bryce, Clara, Drake, and Emily are standing in line for theater tickets. Anna is standing next to Drake. Emily is in front of Anna. Clara is standing between Drake and Bryce. Who is last in line?

(A) Anna (B) Bryce (C) Clara (D) Emily

8. Complete the number sentence. Which property of addition did you use?

$15 + (5 + 38) = (\boxed{} + 5) + 38$

(F) 5; associative **(G) 15; associative** (H) 5; commutative (J) 15; commutative

9. 4,075
   + 928
   (A) 4,993 **(B) 5,003** (C) 5,093 (D) 5,993

10. 26,714
    + 33,525
    (F) 59,239 **(G) 60,239** (H) 69,239 (J) 160,239

11. 18,004
    − 7,106
    (A) 10,898 (B) 10,998 (C) 10,902 (D) 11,102

12. Simplify the expression.
    $(16 - 4) + (12 - 1)$ (F) 33 (G) 25 **(H) 23** (J) 1

13. Find the value of y when $x = 2$ for the following equation.
    $y = 10 - x$ (A) 5 **(B) 8** (C) 12 (D) 20

14. Solve the equation.
    $m + 5 = 15$ (F) 3 **(G) 10** (H) 20 (J) 75

15. Marcy bought a sandwich for $4.19 and a glass of milk for $0.89. How much change should she get back from a $20 bill?
    (A) $14.92 (B) $14.98 (C) $15.08 (D) $15.92

100

Quarterly Test 1

Name _____ Date _____

Find each product.

16. $4 \times 8 = \boxed{}$ (F) 12 (G) 24 (H) 28 **(J) 32**

17. $8 \times 5 = \boxed{}$ (A) 13 **(B) 40** (C) 45 (D) 50

18. $7 \times 6 = \boxed{}$ (F) 13 (G) 36 **(H) 42** (J) 56

Find each quotient and remainder.

19. $45 \div 8 = \boxed{}$ **(A) 5 R5** (B) 5 R3 (C) 4 R5 (D) 4 R3

20. $38 \div 9 = \boxed{}$ (F) 3 R2 (G) 3 R7 **(H) 4 R2** (J) 4 R7

21. $19 \div 4 = \boxed{}$ (A) 3 R7 (B) 4 R1 **(C) 4 R3** (D) 5 R1

22. Solve the equation. Name the property that you used.
    $(9 \times 8) \times 5 = a \times (8 \times 5)$
    (F) 9; Associative Property (G) 9; Commutative Property
    (H) 5; Associative Property (J) 5; Commutative Property

23. Evaluate the expression when $k = 6$.
    $5k - 3$ (A) 6 (B) 12 (C) 24 **(D) 27**

24. Solve.
    $n \div 8 = 7$ (F) 54 **(G) 56** (H) 57 (J) not possible

25. William saved $8 this week. If he continues to save the same amount for 6 weeks, how much will he have altogether?
    (A) $2 (B) $14 (C) $24 **(D) $48**

101

Quarterly Test 2

Name _____ Date _____

Choose the correct answer for each.

Multiply.

1. 5,000
   × 300
   (A) 15,000 (B) 150,000 **(C) 1,500,000** (D) 15,000,000

2. 74
   × 8
   (F) 562 (G) 592 (H) 862 (J) 5,632

3. 837
   × 4
   (A) 3,348 (B) 3,528 (C) 3,548 (D) 321,228

4. $408
   × 7
   (F) $28,056 (G) $28,506 (H) $20,856 **(J) $2,856**

5. 8,000
   × 7
   (A) 5,600 **(B) 56,000** (C) 560,000 (D) 5,600,000

6. 56
   × 21
   (F) 168 (G) 1,168 **(H) 1,176** (J) 11,256

7. 659
   × 35
   (A) 2,365 (B) 5,272 **(C) 23,065** (D) 484,072

8. Which operation would you use to solve the following problem?
   Six friends each want 3 slices of pizza. How many pieces should they order?
   (F) addition (G) subtraction **(H) multiplication** (J) division

Divide.

9. $6\overline{)72}$
   (A) 1 R12 (B) 10 R12 (C) 11 R12 **(D) 12**

10. $4\overline{)2,400}$
    (F) 6 (G) 60 **(H) 600** (J) 6,000

102

Quarterly Test 2

Name _____ Date _____

Divide.

11. $8\overline{)956}$
    (A) 17 (B) 117 **(C) 119 R4** (D) 122

12. $7\overline{)3,009}$
    (F) 44 R1 **(G) 429 R6** (H) 4,029 R6 (J) 4,287

13. Which number is divisible by 2, 5, and 10?
    (A) 30 (B) 35 (C) 55 (D) all of these

14. Which list contains only prime numbers?
    (F) 2, 4, 6, 8, 10 (G) 2, 3, 5, 7, 9 (H) 3, 5, 7, 9, 11 **(J) 2, 3, 5, 7, 11**

15. Find the average of the following numbers.
    40, 44, 45, 50, 51
    (A) 11 (B) 45 **(C) 46** (D) 48

16. Dora is packaging pens. She has 38 pens to package. If 8 pens fit in each package, how many will she have left over?
    (F) 0 (G) 4 **(H) 6** (J) 8

17. The fourth grade class is planning a picnic at the end of the year. They will use vans to transport everyone to the picnic area. There are 30 students in the class. Each van holds 5 students. How many vans will they need?
    (A) 6 (B) 25 (C) 35 (D) 150

Choose the missing number.

18. 4 miles = $\boxed{}$ feet
    (F) 21,120 (G) 8,000 (H) 4,000 (J) 1,320

103

Answer Key

Choose the missing number.

19. 12 cm = ▨ mm
- (A) 120
- (B) 1,200
- (C) 12,000
- (D) 12,000,000

20. 8 pounds = ▨ ounces
- (F) 2
- (G) 16
- (H) 80
- (J) 128

21. 12 feet = ▨ yards
- (A) 2
- (B) 3
- (C) 4
- (D) 6

22. 5,000 milliliters = ▨ liters
- (F) 5
- (G) 500
- (H) 5,000
- (J) 5,000,000

23. 4 gallons = ▨ quarts
- (A) 2
- (B) 8
- (C) 16
- (D) 24

24. What is the temperature?
- (F) 12° C
- (G) 8° C
- (H) ⁻8° C
- (J) ⁻12° C

25. The temperature in Seattle was 56° F when Jenna called Mitchell in New York. Mitchell told her that the temperature was 19° cooler in New York than in Seattle. What was the temperature in New York?
- (A) 37° F
- (B) 43° F
- (C) 47° F
- (D) 75° F

Choose the correct answer for each.

1. Find $\frac{3}{4}$ of 12.
- (A) 8
- (B) 9
- (C) 36
- (D) 48

2. Which mixed number is the same as $\frac{23}{4}$?
- (F) $5\frac{4}{3}$
- (G) $5\frac{3}{4}$
- (H) $5\frac{1}{4}$
- (J) $2\frac{3}{4}$

3. Which fraction is the same as $\frac{12}{18}$ in simplest form?
- (A) $\frac{1}{7}$
- (B) $\frac{1}{3}$
- (C) $\frac{2}{3}$
- (D) $\frac{4}{6}$

Which symbol makes each statement true?

4. $\frac{7}{16}$ ● $\frac{9}{16}$
- (F) >
- (G) <
- (H) =
- (J) +

5. $\frac{4}{12}$ ● $\frac{7}{21}$
- (A) >
- (B) <
- (C) =
- (D) +

Add or subtract. Write the sum or difference in simplest form.

6.
$$\frac{3}{8}$$
$$+\frac{1}{8}$$
- (F) $\frac{1}{2}$
- (G) $\frac{1}{4}$
- (H) $\frac{1}{3}$
- (J) $\frac{4}{8}$

7.
$$4\frac{5}{6}$$
$$-3\frac{1}{6}$$
- (A) $2\frac{2}{3}$
- (B) $1\frac{2}{3}$
- (C) $1\frac{4}{6}$
- (D) $\frac{2}{3}$

8. Andrew, Beth, Clark, and Dana are sitting at a round table. Andrew is not sitting next to Beth. Who is sitting next to Clark?
- (F) Andrew and Dana
- (G) Dana and Beth
- (H) Andrew and Beth
- (J) Only Dana

9. Which fraction or mixed number is the same as 3.25?
- (A) $3\frac{2}{5}$
- (B) $3\frac{25}{100}$
- (C) $3\frac{1}{25}$
- (D) $\frac{3}{25}$

10. Which decimal number is the same as $5\frac{42}{100}$?
- (F) 0.0542
- (G) 0.542
- (H) 5.42
- (J) 54.2

Which symbol makes each statement true?

11. 8.12 ● 8.3
- (A) >
- (B) <
- (C) =
- (D) +

12. 2.500 ● 2.5
- (F) >
- (G) <
- (H) =
- (J) +

13.
$$15.28$$
$$+12.07$$
- (A) 27.35
- (B) 27.45
- (C) 28.25
- (D) 37.25

14.
$$456.19$$
$$-318.47$$
- (F) 137.72
- (G) 138.72
- (H) 142.32
- (J) 148.72

15.
$$21.05$$
$$-13.27$$
- (A) 12.88
- (B) 12.82
- (C) 8.78
- (D) 7.78

16. Round 56.3495 to the nearest tenth.
- (F) 56.2
- (G) 56.3
- (H) 56.34
- (J) 56.35

17. Dennis bought a 3.35-pound package of ground turkey. His recipe calls for 5 pounds of ground turkey. How much more does he need?
- (A) 8.35 pounds
- (B) 2.35 pounds
- (C) 1.35 pounds
- (D) 1.65 pounds

Order the data from least to greatest. Find the range, mode, median, and mean. Then identify any outliers.

18. 9, 6, 6, 4, 2, 3
- (F) range = 4, mode = 6, median = 5, mean = 6, no outliers
- (G) range = 7, mode = 6, median = 5, mean = 6, outlier = 9
- (H) range = 7, mode = 6, median = 5, mean = 7, outlier = 9
- (J) range = 7, mode = 6, median = 5, mean = 5, no outliers

19. 20, 5, 25, 35, 25
- (A) range = 5, mode = 25, median = 25, mean = 25, outlier = 20
- (B) range = 5, mode = 25, median = 25, mean = 22, outlier = 5
- (C) range = 30, mode = 25, median = 25, mean = 22, outlier = 5
- (D) range = 30, mode = 25, median = 25, mean = 22, outlier = 20

Use the graph for Questions 20 and 21.

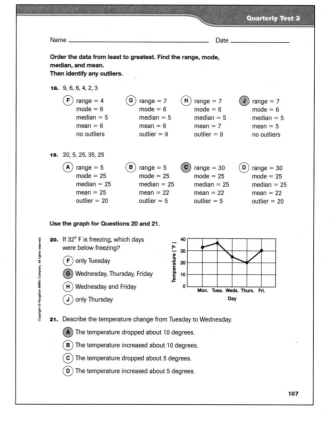

20. If 32° F is freezing, which days were below freezing?
- (F) only Tuesday
- (G) Wednesday, Thursday, Friday
- (H) Wednesday and Friday
- (J) only Thursday

21. Describe the temperature change from Tuesday to Wednesday.
- (A) The temperature dropped about 10 degrees.
- (B) The temperature increased about 10 degrees.
- (C) The temperature dropped about 5 degrees.
- (D) The temperature increased about 5 degrees.

Quarterly Test 3

Name _____ Date _____

A bag contains 3 blue marbles, 1 red marble, and 6 yellow marbles. Choose certain, likely, unlikely, or impossible for Questions 22 and 23.

22. What is the probability of choosing a white marble from the bag?

(F) certain   (G) likely   (H) unlikely   (**J**) impossible

23. What is the probability of choosing a yellow marble from the bag?

(A) certain   (**B**) likely   (C) unlikely   (D) impossible

You write each of the letters C, H, O, O, S, E, O, N, and E on a card and place the cards in a bag.

24. If you pick one card without looking, which cards will you probably pick the most often?

(F) C and E   (G) C and O   (**H**) O and E   (J) C, O, and E

25. If you pick a card and put it back 27 times, how many times would you probably pick the letter H?

(**A**) 3 times   (B) 9 times   (C) 12 times   (D) 27 times

108

Quarterly Test 4

Name _____ Date _____

Choose the correct name for the figure.

1. (A) equilateral triangle   (B) acute scalene triangle
(**C**) right scalene triangle   (D) right isosceles triangle

2. (**F**) parallelogram   (G) rectangle
(H) square   (J) trapezoid

3. How many lines of symmetry does this figure have?

(A) 1   (B) 2
(C) 3   (**D**) 4

4. Find the perimeter of this figure.

8 cm   3 cm   3 cm   12 cm

(F) 20   (**G**) 26
(H) 24   (J) 36

5. Find the perimeter of the square.

26 in.

(A) 26 in.   (B) 52 in.
(**C**) 104 in.   (D) 208 in.

6. Find the area of the rectangle.

38 m   10 m   10 m   38 m

(F) 48 m²   (G) 192 m²
(H) 96 m²   (**J**) 380 m²

109

Quarterly Test 4

Name _____ Date _____

Use this figure for Questions 7 and 8.

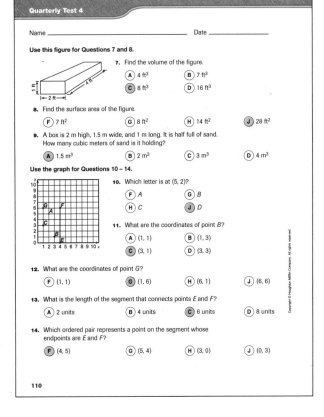

7. Find the volume of the figure.

(A) 4 ft³   (B) 7 ft³
(**C**) 8 ft³   (D) 16 ft³

8. Find the surface area of the figure.

(F) 7 ft²   (G) 8 ft²   (H) 14 ft²   (**J**) 28 ft²

9. A box is 2 m high, 1.5 m wide, and 1 m long. It is half full of sand. How many cubic meters of sand is it holding?

(**A**) 1.5 m³   (B) 2 m³   (C) 3 m³   (D) 4 m³

Use the graph for Questions 10 – 14.

10. Which letter is at (5, 2)?

(F) A   (G) B
(H) C   (**J**) D

11. What are the coordinates of point B?

(A) (1, 1)   (**B**) (1, 3)
(C) (3, 1)   (D) (3, 3)

12. What are the coordinates of point G?

(F) (1, 1)   (**G**) (1, 6)   (H) (6, 1)   (J) (6, 6)

13. What is the length of the segment that connects points E and F?

(A) 2 units   (**B**) 4 units   (C) 6 units   (D) 8 units

14. Which ordered pair represents a point on the segment whose endpoints are E and F?

(**F**) (4, 5)   (G) (5, 4)   (H) (3, 0)   (J) (0, 3)

110

Quarterly Test 4

Name _____ Date _____

Use the number line for Questions 15 and 16. Write the integer for the given letter on the number line.

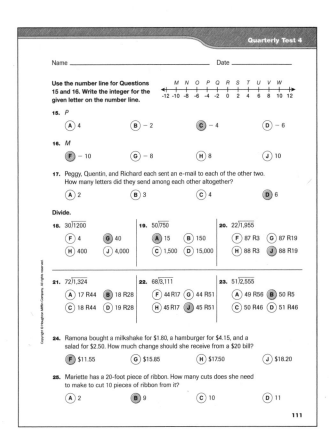

M N O P Q R S T U V W
-12 -10 -8 -6 -4 -2 0 2 4 6 8 10 12

15. P

(A) 4   (B) – 2   (**C**) – 4   (D) – 6

16. M

(**F**) – 10   (G) – 8   (H) 8   (J) 10

17. Peggy, Quentin, and Richard each sent an e-mail to each of the other two. How many letters did they send among each other altogether?

(A) 2   (B) 3   (C) 4   (**D**) 6

Divide.

18. 30)1200

(F) 4   (**G**) 40
(H) 400   (J) 4,000

19. 50)750

(**A**) 15   (B) 150
(C) 1,500   (D) 15,000

20. 22)1,955

(F) 87 R3   (G) 87 R19
(H) 88 R3   (**J**) 88 R19

21. 72)1,324

(**A**) 17 R44   (B) 18 R28
(C) 18 R44   (D) 19 R28

22. 68)3,111

(F) 44 R17   (G) 44 R51
(**H**) 45 R17   (J) 45 R51

23. 51)2,555

(A) 49 R56   (**B**) 50 R5
(C) 50 R46   (D) 51 R46

24. Ramona bought a milkshake for $1.80, a hamburger for $4.15, and a salad for $2.50. How much change should she receive from a $20 bill?

(**F**) $11.55   (G) $15.85   (H) $17.50   (J) $18.20

25. Mariette has a 20-foot piece of ribbon. How many cuts does she need to make to cut 10 pieces of ribbon from it?

(A) 2   (**B**) 9   (C) 10   (D) 11

111

161

Answer Key

Name _____ Date _____

Write the correct answer.

1. Compare 426,345 and 426,305. Use <, >, or =.

426,345 > **426,305**

2. Round 872,568 to the nearest hundred thousand.

900,000

3. Add.

```
  6,463
+   349
  6,812
```

4. Subtract.

```
 15,156
−  6,248
  8,908
```

5. Subtract.

23,000 − 5,020 =

17,980

6. Simplify.

(16 + 3) + (18 − 2) =

35

7. Solve the equation. Name the property that you used.

$7 \times 8 = m \times 7$

8 ; Commutative

8. Evaluate the expression

$24 \div n$ when $n = 6$.

4

Multiply.

9.
```
  308
×   7
2,156
```

10.
```
   45
×  26
1,170
```

Divide.

11. $6\overline{)2,922}$ = **487**

12. Which number is prime?

6   9   13   18

13

13. Find the perimeter of the figure.

5 ft × 6 ft

22 ft

112

Name _____ Date _____

14. Fill in the missing number.

24 inches = **2** feet

15. Write the mixed number for the improper fraction.

$\frac{9}{7}$ $1\frac{2}{7}$

16. Add. Write the sum in simplest form.

$\frac{3}{8} + \frac{1}{8} =$ **$\frac{1}{2}$**

17. Subtract. Write the difference in simplest form.

$\frac{11}{12} - \frac{9}{12} =$ **$\frac{1}{6}$**

18. Compare 3.09 and 3.9. Use <, >, or =. **3.09 < 3.9**

19. Add.

```
  6.3
+ 5.9
 12.2
```

20. Subtract.

```
 15.4
−  9.6
  5.8
```

21. Order the data from least to greatest. Find the range, mode, median, and mean.

6   9   4   6   5

4, 5, 6, 6, 9

range = 5; mode = 6; median = 6; mean = 6

22. Name the figure.

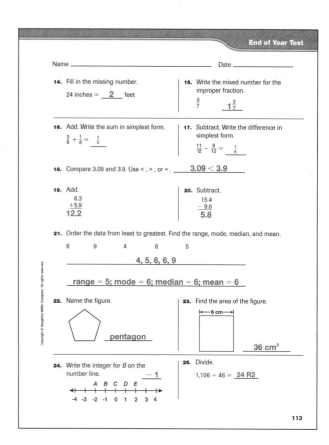

pentagon

23. Find the area of the figure.

6 cm

36 cm²

24. Write the integer for *B* on the number line.

−1

```
  A  B  C  D  E
+--+--+--+--+--+--+--+--+--
-4 -3 -2 -1  0  1  2  3  4
```

25. Divide.

1,106 ÷ 46 = **24 R2**

113

162

DATE DUE

FEB 2 0 2012